Pauline in a new hat, during her first triumphant visit to London, England.

Pauline Johnson
Her
Life and Work

Presented To :

Mrs Mickey Rota

With sincere appreciation
for your dedicated ministry
as Primary Superintendent of
our Church School.

Bridge Street United Church

Don Leslie
(Gen, Supt)

Pauline Johnson
Her Life and Work

Her biography
written by

Her prose & poems
selected by

Marcus Van Steen

MUSSON BOOK COMPANY • TORONTO

🌷 *By the same author*

LEGENDS OF VANCOUVER
written by Pauline Johnson
compiled by Marcus Van Steen

Copyright © 1965

MUSSON BOOK COMPANY
a division of
HODDER & STOUGHTON LTD. TORONTO

Set in 12 pt. Linotype Granjon, 1 pt. leaded
Design & Calligraphy by Anthony Lovell

Printed and bound in Canada by
JOHN DEYELL LIMITED LINDSAY ONTARIO

❧ CONTENTS

❦ Contents *(Continued)*

POETRY *(continued)*

❦ Contents *(Continued)*

❧ Contents *(Continued)*

It is difficult, in making a reassessment of the work of E. Pauline Johnson, to strike a fair balance between the adulation that was meted out to her before and after her death, in 1913, and the comparative neglect that has been her lot in recent years. From a present-day point of view, her poetry was over-praised by her contemporaries. One is led to suspect that the praise so often bestowed was evoked not so much by her literary work as by her vibrant personality and her considerable charm. In addition there was the romance of her birth, with its Mohawk Indian background, the gay freedom of her way of life, and the tragedy of her premature death — all of which combined to weave an aura of splendour around her person and her work. Two generations later, the splendour has dimmed and the magic no longer casts its spell. For today's readers it is necessary to separate the legend from the reality, in order to assess Miss Johnson's place in Canadian history and her contribution to our literature.

EMILY PAULINE JOHNSON was born on March 10th, 1861, on the Six Nations Reservation near

Brantford, Ontario. On her father's side she was of a noble Mohawk family, bearing a title that dated back to the days of Hiawatha and the fifty Indian leaders who created the League of the Iroquois some half-century before Columbus first crossed the Atlantic. Her family name was Tekahionwake, which means "double Wampum". The name "Johnson" was acquired from the British colonial leader, Sir William Johnson, who acted as godfather to Pauline's great-grandfather when he was baptized into the Christian faith at Niagara, in New York State, a few years before the American Revolution. At such baptisms Indian families usually adopted English names, and the fact that the great Sir William offered his name to the lad, who was baptized Jacob Johnson, is an indication of the prominence of the Tekahionwake family.

Jacob's son was called Sakayengwaraton, which may be translated as "the early morning mist of Indian Summer", and he was generally called Smoke Johnson. A hero of the War of 1812, he served with Sir Isaac Brock at Queenston Heights, and later took part in such engagements as Stoney Creek, Beaver Dams and Lundy's Lane. Smoke Johnson married Helen Martin, a daughter of the notable Mohawk chieftain George Martin and Catherine Rolleston, a white girl of German descent who had been carried off during an Indian raid on a Pennsylvania settlement and brought up as an Indian. The Smoke Johnsons had a son, George Henry Martin Johnson, Pauline's father. He carried on the family tradition as a Mohawk chieftain, but could not pass the chieftainship on to his sons because he married a white girl, Emily Susanna Howells, sister-in-law of the Anglican missionary on the Brantford Reservation. This barrier did not apply in the case of his grandmother, Catherine Rolleston, because she had been formally and properly adopted into the Mohawk nation — had taken out her citizenship papers, as it were.

🌺 2

Chief Johnson and his English wife had four children, Henry Beverly, Evelyn, Allen and Emily Pauline. Because of her English mother and her German great-grandmother, Pauline was more than half white, a fact which never kept her from proclaiming herself wholly Indian, as she was by law, by temperament, and by choice.

"I am a Red Indian and feel very proud of it," she told a London reporter on her first visit to England in 1894. "I love everything Indian."

One of Pauline's many friends, the Canadian naturalist and writer, Ernest Thompson Seton, has recorded her as saying: "There are those who think they pay me a compliment by saying I am just like a white woman. I am Indian, and my aim, my joy and my pride is to sing the glories of my own people. Ours was the race that gave the world its measure of heroism, its standard of physical prowess. Ours was the race that taught the world that avarice veiled by any other name is crime, and ours was the faith that taught men to live without greed and to die without fear."

In taking this stand, Pauline was actually paying tribute to her splendid mother who defied her family and many of her English friends to stand by the side of the young Mohawk chieftain who had won her heart. The story of this romance is told by Pauline in her short story called simply *My Mother*. This account is fiction only because the names have been lightly disguised. Emily Howells, for example, becomes Lydia Bestman. The Reverend Mr. Elliott becomes the Reverend Mr. Evans, and the young Mohawk warrior becomes George Mansion — derived from the name bestowed on George Johnson when he became chief, which was On-Wan-On-Syshon, meaning "Great House" or "Mansion". But although the names were changed, the story as told by Miss Johnson is history, the history of her remarkable family. More particularly, it was the history of her mother. As Miss

Johnson said, in a note appended to the story when it was first published: "This is the story of my mother's life, every incident of which she related to me herself. I have neither exaggerated nor curtailed a single circumstance. I have supplied nothing through imagination, nor have I heightened the colouring of her unusual experiences." As portrayed by Pauline, in this story and frequently in other accounts of her childhood, her mother was serene and happy in her choice and determined that her children "should be reared as Indians in spirit and patriotism", loving the Indian legends, the Indian habits and customs, the Indian people themselves.

Pauline had little patience with those who persisted in expressing amazement concerning her Mohawk blood. On her last crossing to England in 1907 an American lady on board ship said to her one day: "Excuse me, Miss Johnson, but was your father a real Indian?" Pauline said that he was and the lady replied: "I am surprised. You don't look the least bit like it." Pauline then asked: "And was your father a real white man?" Indignantly, the lady declared that of course he was white. "Well," said Pauline sweetly, "I am equally surprised."

Pauline was also annoyed when some critics persisted in attributing her talent to the Howells strain, on the grounds that the Ohio branch of the family produced the great nineteenth century novelist of social comment, William Dean Howells. However, to compare Pauline with her famous cousin is like comparing a carefree, singing child to a bearded philosopher. W. D. Howells was concerned with the details of life, which he dissected with careful logic. Pauline, on the other hand, experienced life, and sang for the same reasons that she laughed and wept. In her best work, her use of metaphor, her ability to express colour, light and shade, and her use of vivid and compelling imagery, indicate that she owed much to her grandfather, Smoke Johnson, who was a famous orator, known far and wide as "The Mohawk Warbler."

The only time Pauline ever mentioned her novelist cousin in connection with her work concerned one of her early poems, *In The Shadows*. "I sent this poem to no fewer than eleven American magazines," she said, "and during its travels Mr. Howells got hold of it and criticized it severely. At last, however, the poem was published in *The Athenaeum* of London, perhaps the severest, most critical publication in the world. I drew a circle around the poem and sent the magazine to Mr. Howells, but of course he never acknowledged it."

'CHIEFSWOOD'

As the youngest child of a close and affectionate family, Pauline appears to have been thoroughly pampered from her earliest infancy. The home she grew up in was a fine, big, stuccoed colonial mansion set in a well-wooded park over-looking the Grand River. This estate, called 'Chiefswood', was prepared by George Henry Martin Johnson for his bride, and furnished in a manner which the young warrior imagined would make his English wife feel happily at home, including a piano, which was a rare luxury even in white homes of Upper Canada in 1853. The well-stocked library included such contemporary favourites as Dickens and Carlyle as well as the accepted classics. Chief Johnson spoke and read German and French as well as English, Mohawk and the five other languages of the Six Nations — knowledge which earned for him the position of Official Interpreter on the Reservation as well as interpreter for the Anglican mission. Mrs. Johnson had a fine, intelligent mind, enhanced by her upbringing and her devotion to good literature.

Such a home and such a couple inevitably attracted visitors. The lengthy guest-list at 'Chiefswood' included the

Marquis of Lorne and the Princess Louise, Lord and Lady Dufferin, General Sir Garnet Wolseley, and a number of scholars and writers. Among these was the eminent anthropologist, Horatio Hale, who has given us this picture of 'Chiefswood': "The elegent and tasteful Indian home in the tree-embowered mansion overlooking the winding river, the cordial and dignified chief, the gentle English matron and the graceful and accomplished young Princesses — all making a picture so charming that visitors to Brantford, famous writers, actors and other public figures, eagerly sought an introduction there".

Another guest who has left us his impressions was the Canadian artist, Homer Watson, who visited 'Chiefswood' with three friends in 1879. "The Chief and his cultured wife made us welcome," he recalled. "Pauline and her sister sang duets, and then Pauline, a slight, striking-looking young girl, recited some of her verses, which showed much talent."

From an early age Pauline displayed a fondness for poetry. There is a story of a guest at 'Chiefswood' asking the nine-year-old girl what treat she would like him to bring her on his next visit, and being surprised when she asked for a book of verse. She herself wrote that "by the time I was twelve I had read every line Scott ever wrote, every line of Longfellow, much of Byron, Shakespeare and Emerson." Browsing happily through the excellent library at 'Chiefswood', she had also dipped into most of the prose writers, from Addison to Macaulay.

There is no doubt that her interest in poetry was encouraged by her mother, who read Keats and Byron rather than Mother Goose to her babies in their cradles, and was always proud of her ability to memorise poetry. In an interview with Isabel Ecclestone Mackay in Vancouver some months before her death, Pauline said that her mother once exclaimed to her: "Pauline, you say in your verses exactly what I have so often felt but never could express".

Over the years, her mother had made fugitive attempts to write poetry. Among the papers Pauline left behind were two scraps in her mother's delicate handwriting. One, dated April 12, 1845, contains two eight-line verses entitled *To A Friend*, written in the style made famous by the Irish poet Thomas Moore:

> *"When years have rolled o'er thee,*
> *And pleasures have fled,*
> *And this comes before thee*
> *Like one from the dead......."*

The other, dated Valentine's Day, 1853, and signed "from your devoted Valentine," starts out:

> *"Forget me not, 'tis all I ask*
> *In this lone world, of thee;*
> *Though far apart we ply our task,*
> *Oh, sometimes think of me."*

Always a favourite of her mother, Pauline was educated mainly at home. For two years she had a governess, but most of her early training was received from her mother, who introduced her to the various mysteries of household management as well as to the glories and pleasures of discriminating reading. Another close companion of her childhood days was her grandfather, Smoke Johnson, who indoctrinated her with the history of past Indian greatness and the legends of her father's people. An accomplished story-teller and orator, the old chief — he was seventy when his grand-daughter was born — could make the long saga of the Six Nations live for the intense little girl. In her later life Pauline always spoke with great reverence and love for her distinguished grandparent.

❦ 7

Pauline also managed to enjoy a fairly close relationship with her father, in spite of many difficulties. Besides the obvious handicap of official business, which frequently took her father away from home, there was the added problem that for many years before his death Chief Johnson was physically a broken man. When Pauline was four, her father was attacked and brutally beaten by a gang of thugs who resented his efforts to put an end to the traffic in raw whisky on the Reservation. He never completely recovered from the injuries he received at that time, and there is no doubt they hastened his untimely end.

Pauline remembered her father chiefly for the occasional walks on which she accompanied him through the Reservation, when he aroused her interest in, and love for, the plants and trees, the wild birds and animals. One time they rescued a baby chipmunk whose mother had been killed, and she kept it as a pet for several years. For many years also her constant companion was a little black spaniel "Chips" which was a gift from her father, and outlived him. However, Pauline always regretted that she saw her father much less frequently than she would have wished, and then often only when he was accompanied by guests.

It is possible that this type of gracious home life, the close companionship of cultured and indulgent elders, and the frequent visits of outstanding and brilliant men and women, provided her with a better education than she could have got anywhere else. Certainly she received very little formal schooling. Her total school career lasted only five years — three years at an Indian day school on the Reservation, and two years at the Central Collegiate in Brantford.

Pauline was sixteen when she started to attend the Brantford school. At that time David Curtis, the Collector of Customs in Brantford, was a friend of Chief Johnson. When the Chief and Mrs. Johnson mentioned that they wished

Pauline to go to school for a time in Brantford, the Curtises suggested that she live with them. Pauline would have to stay somewhere in Brantford as "Chiefswood" was eighteen miles distant from the school. It was Pauline's first experience away from home, and for the first time she had the companionship of girls her own age. She attended school with a young daughter of her new household, Emily Curtis, and it was at the Curtis home that Pauline met Jean Morton, whom she cherished as a firm and intimate friend for many years. It was to Jean that Pauline dedicated her first published poem, and there is no doubt that the two girls were very much attached to each other.

In the year that Pauline started going to school, 1877, Brantford achieved city status, with a population of about 10,000. It was a cosmopolitan population, as Brantford then was among the leading half-dozen industrial cities of Canada, with busy factories eager to employ many of the newly-arrived immigrants from overseas. These factories turned out a wide range of goods, from farm equipment and steam engines to pottery and paper products. The factory owners, the managers, the city's professional men, mostly of British stock, lived in solid, white-brick homes on the wide, tree-lined residential streets. On market days, three times a week, there was a further mingling of population when the Indians, who still spoke mainly their own languages, arrived in town from the Reservation to sell their farm products in the open-air market around the City Hall steps in the heart of the bustling community. The markets in those days were picturesque affairs, with the beaded buckskins and feathers of the Indians, the gay head-scarves, the brightly-decorated skirts of the European women, the huge baskets of bright red tomatoes (twenty-five cents a bushel) or the glistening apples (fifty cents a bushel), the squawking chickens being sold live (two for fifty cents), and the babel of conflicting languages.

❦ 9

The school which Pauline attended still stands on Sheri-
dan street, and some of the books that were hers in those days
are now on display in the Brant Historical Museum in Brantford. On the fly-leaf of one book, over the date November 8,
1877, we find the new student experimenting with two different signatures, E. Pauline Johnson and Pauline E. Johnson.
In spite of her baptismal name, no one ever called her Emily.
Her friends always called her Pauline, sometimes shortened
to Pauley or Paul. Her formal signature remained *E. Pauline
Johnson*, although after her first visit to London in 1894,
when she fully realized what an important asset her Mohawk
inheritance could be, we find her adding *Tekahionwake* to
her signature, at times hyphenating it with the Johnson, or
sometimes adding it in parenthesis underneath.

On her first arrival at the Central Collegiate, Pauline was
a shy and serious girl, with her long black hair worn in a
braid down her back. Her large, expressive eyes, shining
from her dark-skinned face, were lively and observant,
always on the alert. There is no doubt, as she later described
many of the Indian children in her stories, that she was on
the defensive about her mixed ancestry. But Pauline's way
was to glory in her difference, and it is obvious that she was
generally accepted for what she herself was. As she got to
know people better, she relaxed into lively playfulness, and
we find her inviting several of her young friends for week-
ends at 'Chiefswood'.

Much as she loved companionship, there were times when
Pauline preferred to be alone. At such times she might disappear into her room with a pile of books and spend hours
reading omnivorously, or studying her school work. It is
interesting to note that during her two years at the Central
Collegiate she got high marks in all subjects except mathe-
matics. At other times she would take her canoe out on the
Grand River, paddle for a while upstream and then float

leisurely down again with a book in her hands and the sun on her back. While thus engaged, Pauline was Indian enough to scorn any suggestion that she carry a parasol as other young ladies of her class would have done in those days when every device was used to preserve a milk-white complexion. That is probably why every description of Pauline mentions her dark Indian skin although were she living today her complexion would probably not be noticeably dark alongside the golden-tan look that has become fashionable.

There were times, too, when she would temporarily forget her new-found friends and return to her Indian past. It was then that she would visit her grandfather, Chief Smoke Johnson, who helped her keep alive her knowledge of the Mohawk language as he stirred her imagination with vivid tales about the great past of her father's people.

Pauline was also very close to her two brothers, and eagerly looked forward to the Christmas holidays when her elder brother Beverly would be home from Hellmuth College. She was very proud of Beverly, of his good looks and his splendid scholastic record, but most of all she was proud of his skill on the piano. While he was at home she would invite several of her closest friends to visit, when the fine big house would ring with music, singing and laughter. Another of her favourite Christmas pastimes was to go hunting for small game with her two brothers and their several dogs.

Two frequent visitors were Jean Morton and Douglas Reville, who later married Jean and became editor of the *Brantford Expositor*. Both have left us descriptions of those happy week-ends, when ten or a dozen close friends gathered at 'Chiefswood'. Pauline was always full of plans for picnics, campfires, sing-songs or canoeing expeditions. The Grand River which swept past 'Chiefswood' was perfect for canoeing in those days, presenting an ever-changing shoreline of high banks crowned with willows or birches, or low meadowland fringed with reeds across which the redwing blackbirds flashed and dipped. Reville describes Pauline as "a most bright and witty companion. To know her best was during one of the canoeing trips she loved so much."

Along with her bubbling gaiety, there was also a strong undercurrent of moody introspection which was obvious to Pauline's friends even at this early age. On the cover of one of her schoolbooks, now in the Brant Historical Museum, we find the sixteen-year-old girl writing:

> *"What though in lonely grief I sigh*
> *For friends beloved no longer nigh,*
> *Submissive still would I reply:*
> *Thy will be done."*

With Beverly and her sister Evelyn away at college so much while Pauline was growing up, she developed a very close relationship with her brother Allen, who was closest to her in age. At 'Chiefswood', which is now maintained as a Pauline Johnson museum, there is a copy of *Flint and Feather*, her last Christmas present to Allen, dedicated in her failing hand: "To my dear brother Allen with the love which has always been the same and the loyalty which has never lessened through all the years that have drifted by since our earliest childhood."

This is signed, and dated "Vancouver, BC Christmas, 1912". Underneath there is scrawled a sort of postscript in which the extreme unevenness of the script may be due partly to emotion as well as to ebbing strength: "With happy memories of countless glorious days of comradeship with canoe and paddle".

All her life, Pauline regarded the canoe as a symbol of carefree happiness, and whenever she felt bruised by the pressures of life she would always try to escape to a patch of open water and a canoe. Her skill with a canoe was admitted, and admired, by experts who said that if she had agreed to enter competition she would have proved herself the top canoe woman in North America. As it was, she was always a welcome guest at the annual meets of the various canoe clubs of Ontario, and even further afield. The Secretary of the American Canoe Club, R. Easton Burns, became her close friend and admirer, and it was at his request that she donated the poem *The Portage* which was featured in the club's Year Book for 1893.

In 1879 Pauline finished her studies at Central School and returned to her life of idleness — and it must be admitted that during this period of her life, Pauline was a very idle young woman indeed. Her father was not a wealthy man, but Pauline had been brought up to a life of ease, in a home where good taste, simplicity and careful management created a gracious atmosphere without the need of a great deal of money. There is no doubt that 'Chiefswood' was run with a good deal of elegance. Even such casual visitors as Jean Morton tell that at every meal the table was graced with gleaming glassware, silver, snowy napkins and formal service. This explains how, later, when Pauline visited London she was able to fit easily into fashionable circles and become readily at home.

For five years after leaving school, Pauline was able to live exactly as she chose, and she chose to spend her days in reading a lot, writing a little, enjoying games and good times with her friends, and dreaming away the long golden summer afternoons in her canoe on the Grand River. On several occasions she joined several of her school friends on camping trips into the Muskoka Lake area of Ontario, near Georgian Bay, and was awed and impressed by its tremendous natural beauty. Muskoka became one of Pauline's favourite places. Many years after those camping trips she wrote several poems which indicate how longingly she looked back on those carefree days when she relaxed with her friends in the midst of some of the best scenery in Canada.

Those halcyon days of dream-filled idleness came to an abrupt end in 1884, when Pauline was twenty-three. After several years of broken health, her father died and the bereaved family found it could not afford the upkeep of 'Chiefswood'. The widow with her two daughters moved to lodgings in Brantford, where Evelyn secured an office job with the Indian Office. The two boys had already left home to go to work, one in Hamilton and the other in Toronto. Pauline, for the first time in her life, was brought face to face with the problem of earning her living.

FIRST FLIGHTS

During this period, Pauline found a new strength, helped and encouraged by her two most intimate friends, Jean Morton and Douglas Reville. Her tribute to Jean is contained in lines written in her friend's autograph book:

My Jeanie:
> *When thou art near*
> *The sweetest joys still sweeter seem,*
> *The brightest hopes more bright appear,*
> *And life is all one happy dream,*
> *When thou art near.*

Reville, speaking with the new authority of a young man already well established at the Brantford *Expositor*, urged Pauline to send out some of her poems to well-recognized literary magazines. He mentions particularly the one she had written for Jean a few years before, *My Little Jean*, which became Pauline's first published poem, appearing in *Gems of Poetry*, of New York in 1885.

Gems of Poetry edited by John Douglas, formerly of the Montreal *Witness*, also published Pauline's second poem,

The Fourth Act, which also saw the first light of day in Jean's autograph book.

Before either of these were published, Pauline and her sister were invited to Buffalo, New York, to take the place of their dead father at ceremonies connected with the re-interment of the famous Seneca orator, Red Jacket, and eight other Seneca chiefs, whose graves were in danger of desecration by builders. The Buffalo Historical Society had secured a permanent burial ground in the Forest Lawn Cemetery in that city, and on October 9th, 1884, reburied Chief Red Jacket and his Seneca brethren with appropriate ceremony. Pauline contributed a moving poem which was used on the occasion. This is the first poem Pauline wrote in which she boasted of her Indian lineage and expressed sympathy with her Indian forbears. The key lines:

> *"And few today remain:*
> *But copper-tinted face and smoldering fire*
> *Of wilder life, were left me by my sire*
> *To be my proudest claim."*

were later used in the frontspiece of her first published volume, *The White Wampum*.

In 1886, when Brantford was unveiling a statue to Joseph Brant, the Mohawk chief whose name the city bears, Pauline was asked to contribute a poem, and obliged with a rather formal ode written largely in conventional patriotic terms. It is amusing, in view of her later flamboyant platform appearances, to learn that on this occasion Pauline was too shy to read her poem to the assembled audience, and it was done by a local industrialist, W. F. Cockshutt, later to become a Member of Parliament.

This indicates that Pauline had already made something of a local name for herself as a writer, totally unpaid, of charming and appropriate verses. It was doubtless naive of her, lacking as she was in experience and worldly knowledge, to imagine that she could turn this talent to profitable use, to earn enough to pay her own way and to help support her mother. But this is what she attempted to do. The first Canadian publication to accept her work was *The Week*, the Toronto magazine founded by Goldwin Smith, which bought *A Cry From An Indian Wife* in June 1885. The editor of *The Week* at that time was Charles G. D. Roberts, less than a year older than Pauline but already the author of an impressive body of poetical work, including his first book, *Orion*, published five years previously. Pauline, in other words, was starting out on a poetical career at an age when most poets are getting their second wind. Pauline had every reason to regret her protracted and leisurely adolescence, and it may be wondered if Canadian readers in general may not also have cause for regret.

Roberts became a life-long friend of Pauline, and among her books now on display at "Chiefswood" is a copy of his *Land of Evangeline* inscribed "To Miss Pauline Johnson, from her friend and fellow craftsman", and dated 1896.

Another Canadian publication which showed an early appreciation for Pauline's work was *Saturday Night* of Toronto, where one of the junior editorial employees at that time was Hector Charlesworth, later to become Chairman of the Canadian Radio Broadcasting Commission and a good friend to many an aspiring Canadian writer. In his *Candid Chronicles* many years later, Mr. Charlesworth wrote: "Of all the friends of my apprenticeship days, the one who became most famous and certain of a measure of immortality was Emily Pauline Johnson." He also commented: "I never met any native-born Canadian who gave such a complete sense of aristocracy."

By 1889 Pauline was well-enough known to have two of her poems included in *Songs of the Great Dominion*, a poetry anthology compiled by the Montreal lawyer-poet William Douw Lighthall. These poems, *In The Shadows* and *At The Ferry*, were singled out for special praise by the influential English critic Theodore Watts-Dunton, who hailed this appearance of "a poet so rare — so full of the spirit of the open air".

But critical praise was of little use to the fatherless little family in Brantford where Pauline, approaching thirty, was desperately conscious of the fact that, so far from being a help to her mother, she was as dependent as her mother was on the generosity of the other members of the family. Mr Charlesworth once recalled that during this period he made out a pay-slip of $3 for *The Song My Paddle Sings*, without doubt the most famous of Pauline's poems, and he said that this actually was more than most publications of the time paid for poetry.

WIDER HORIZONS

Clearly some new approach was needed, and Pauline found it, or rather had it thrust into her hands. In January, 1892, she was invited to join with a number of other poets in a verse-reading entertainment for the Young Liberal Club of Toronto. The organizer of the literary evening was Frank Yeigh, a journalist prominent in Toronto at the time. Among the poets taking part were Duncan Campbell Scott, W. W. Campbell, W. R. Lighthall and Helen Merrill. As Mr Yeigh wrote later: "The evening was dragging a little, and the interest waning when the Indian poet-princess was introduced. She glided rather than walked to the platform, her dark eyes flashing nervously and her sinewy form the essence of gracefulness, representing the acme of physical rhythm and motion. Then she gave the first rendition of her *Cry From An Indian Wife*. Thrilling was the effect, dramatic the appeal of this dark-hued girl who seemed to personify

❧ 17

her race. A tense stillness followed, but only for a moment. Then there broke unrestrained expressions of approval in tumultuous applause. Rarely does an audience so rapidly change its mood, and rarely does a reciter so capture her hearers. Tekahionwake leaped into fame that night. . . ."

While Mr Yeigh was undoubtedly using a pardonable exaggeration, it may truthfully be said that Miss Johnson leaped into a new career that night — a career that was not only to earn her a livelihood for almost twenty years, but was also to bring her a larger measure of fame during her lifetime than her writings. Those were the days in Canada of the platform entertainer. It was a Canada without motion pictures, without radio or television, too young to have developed an adequate local reservoir of talent in any of the performing arts. First-class theatre was rare, and even then was available usually only in such centres as Toronto and Montreal. For the most part the people depended for entertainment on touring performers — men who gave "dramatic readings" or monologues, women who recited or sang, jugglers, performing dogs, magicians, groups of two or three who presented short excerpts from famous plays. They performed in church halls, in schoolrooms, in "opera houses", in tents, in curtained-off corners of saloons, in any available space that would accommodate a stage, no matter how makeshift, and, certainly of equal importance, an audience. Some of those performers were world-famous artists, from Charles Dickens, who toured North America with readings from his novels in the 1860s, to Sir Harry Lauder in the early years of this century. And between 1892 and 1909, Miss Johnson was one of dozens of platform entertainers who toured Canada from coast to coast, not once but several times. Furthermore, Miss Johnson took her special type of entertainment deep into the United States and on three occasions across the sea to England.

Following the success of her first platform appearance, Mr Yeigh lost no time in arranging for a second performance, and during the next few months Pauline made 125 appearances in Ontario and Quebec, to a growing chorus of acclaim. Before the end of 1892 we find the young woman who was too shy to read a short poem to a gathering of her friends and neighbours in Brantford in 1886 had become a seasoned platform entertainer. There is every indication that, driven on to the public platform by necessity, Pauline found she enjoyed it. She had inherited some of the histrionic flair that had made her grandfather the "Mohawk Warbler". And this, combined with her own natural charm and vivacity, very soon made her one of the most popular touring entertainers in the country. This by itself was enough to make her new way of life very attractive to Pauline, whose racial inheritance and unusual childhood combined to make her unusually desirous of popularity. Never having mixed much with ordinary people until well into her teens, Pauline for most of her life was unsure of acceptance as a person, and she was inclined to be inordinately pleased and grateful when she was assured that she was. Love and acceptance, more than fame and money, were what she demanded from her audiences, and that is a demand few audiences can resist.

A letter Miss Johnson wrote in 1891 is a good indication of her need for approval and reassurance. It was written to A. S. Hardy, a Brantford neighbour, then Provincial Secretary and later to become Prime Minister of Ontario, in reply to a note he sent in praise of her poem *ReVoyage*, which had been printed in the Brantford *Expositor* after appearing in the New York *Independent*. Her letter expresses fulsome thanks for Mr Hardy's notice which "will always be regarded as an imperishable laurel leaf in my tiny wreath." Pauline then adds this significant sentence: "I can scarcely tell you how often an author requires approbation, or how dear is the handclasp of encouragement when it does come."

There was also a certain amount of stubborn pride involved in her determination to continue with her new way of life. Even as late as 1892 there were still many people in Canada who frowned on the idea of a woman taking on a career outside the home. And there were also many who regarded any woman who trod the theatrical boards as definitely not respectable. Always a spirited fighter, Pauline needed only a hint of opposition to arouse her determination to persist and persevere, and in this she was encouraged by her mother who, in her time, had run counter to public opinion.

Too many women had preceded Pauline for her to be regarded as a pioneer in breaking down popular prejudices, but she did her part. And she failed only because the prejudices struck close enough, finally, to poison to a certain extent the last years of her life.

Among those who disapproved strongly of Pauline's chosen way of life was her sister Evelyn, and the gulf between them grew to the point that they ceased communicating with each other. This was a matter of great sadness to Pauline, who had the Indian reverence for family ties. Even her final illness did not entirely break down the barrier between the sisters. Evelyn did go to Vancouver, mainly because she felt it was only proper for some member of the family to be present at a time of death, but after a few painful meetings even Evelyn herself agreed it would be kinder if she curtailed her visits to the sickroom.

Fortunately all this, in 1892, was still too far in the future to cast any shadow over Pauline's delight in her new profession, and one of the main reasons why she was such an instantaneous success as an entertainer was that she did enjoy it so much. She threw herself completely into her readings. In delivering her Indian ballads, she was all savage, her deep

❦ 20

rich voice harsh with blood-lust, her eyes flashing fire, her whole personality suffused with pleasure in her ability to make people's spines tingle with delicious excitement. Then she would change completely for a quiet lyric of the delights of nature, her voice liltingly musical, caressingly smooth, her dark eyes becoming as deep and mysterious as one of her beloved river pools. She was naturally lithe and graceful, the result of many hours of propelling her canoe among the currents of the Grand — for there is no better training for a good posture than learning the skilful handling of a canoe. Also, she had a delightful sense of humour. One of her early concerts was at Penetanguishene, on Georgian Bay, near the famous shrine commemorating the martyrdom of Father Breboeuf and his fellow Jesuits at the hands of the Iroquois. To her audience in the Roman Catholic hall, she calmly introduced herself in these words: "Most of you have never heard of me and I am sure we have never met before, but some of my ancestors met some friends of yours not far from here, some two hundred and forty years ago."

On another occasion, in Cornwall, she was third on a list of five attractions at a concert which was interrupted frequently by a gang of rowdy young men in the balcony. The two performers who preceded Pauline suffered severely from heckling, and left the stage almost in tears of rage and frustration. Pauline was greeted with shrill catcalls from the balcony toughs. As soon as this died down, Pauline said: "When I see a crowd of boys having a good time in the balcony, I am always sorry....."

At this point her words were drowned out by booing and loud satirical groans, the boys no doubt expecting the usual pious reprimand. But when the noise had subsided enough, Pauline went on: "Yes, I am sorry I am not up there with them."

❦ 21

This brought the house down with laughter and applause, and there was no more heckling that night.

LONDON DAYS

From the proceeds of her platform appearances in 1892 and 1893, Pauline was able to go to England in 1894 to arrange for the publication of her first book *The White Wampum*. This was a rich and fruitful literary period, and Pauline's book appeared in very good company. The 1894 Autumn list of Bodley Head, which included *The White Wampum*, also contained new works by Aubrey Beardsley, John Buchan, Edmund Gosse and the Russian novelist Dostoevsky.

The same season also saw new books of verse by Grant Allen, another Canadian, the tragic Francis Thompson, and the great Sir William Watson. Thomas Hardy had just published his *Tess of the D'Urbervilles*, and among the best sellers were Marie Corelli, Conan Doyle, Rider Haggard, Hall Cain and the Canadian-born Sir Gilbert Parker. Robert Louis Stevenson died that year in far-off Samoa, and Oscar Wilde was about to disappear from the scene for a three-year period. Another young Irishman, George Bernard Shaw, was building up a considerable reputation on Fleet Street; H. G. Wells was beginning to stir the reading public with his new novels and outrageous ideas, and J. M. Barrie was bringing a new influence into the English theatre. Pauline's slim volume was moving in every bit as good company as was Pauline herself during that year in London.

Indeed it has been said that no Canadian who had gone to London up to her time had received quite so warm a welcome. Those were the days of the drawing-room entertainment, and Pauline was in great demand throughout the season of 1894. Besides being beautiful and talented, with a warm and attractive personality, Pauline had the novel advantage of being an Indian princess. The London newspapers made the most of this, featuring her Mohawk name and recounting in garbled fashion the exploits of her father and grandfather. One mistake made consistently was to confuse the War of 1812 with the American Revolutionary War, as in most English histories the Canadian-American War of 1812 is crowded out by the catastrophic events of Napoleon's invasion of Russia.

Pauline quickly realized the theatrical appeal of her Indian heritage and appeared frequently in Indian costume, featuring the fringed and beaded buckskins, bear-claw necklace, and beaded moccasins that were later to become familiar on thousands of platforms across Canada. The prominent actor-manager, Sir George Alexander, was so impressed by her Indian background that he wished to have a full-length drama made out of her short story *A Red Girl's Reasoning*, that had been first published in *Dominion Illustrated* in February 1893. This story has as its theme the clash between the Indian and white cultures in North America as illustrated in the marriage of an Indian girl with a young white official who brought her back to Ottawa. But although the story lacked sufficient material to sustain a full-length drama, it made an effective dramatic sketch, and was used by Pauline in that way on later tours of Canada.

To have been such a success in the London of 1894 was a tremendous achievement for an unsophisticated young woman from a small Ontario town. The London of those days was the great Imperial city of Queen Victoria, Prime Minister Gladstone, Sir Julian Huxley, Gilbert and Sullivan, and as brilliant an array of scientists, artists, writers and philosophers as ever graced any world capital. Pauline's way was smoothed, of course, by the fact that some prominent people in London were able to recall visits to 'Chiefswood' and were interested in the success of one of the daughters of

❦ 23

the old Indian chief. Among these was the Duke of Connaught who, as Prince Arthur, had been initiated into the Mohawk nation at a ceremony at 'Chiefswood' in 1869. Years later, when the Duke was Governor-General of Canada, he interrupted a tour of British Columbia to spend half-an-hour at the death-bed of Pauline Johnson — a simple gesture that brightened her final days.

The White Wampum was a critical success, but though it brought Pauline considerable fame, it did not earn her very much money. It made editors anxious to use her work, but did not make them any more willing to pay for it. Even such a well-established magazine as *Rod and Gun* felt justified in sending Pauline a cheque for 75 cents for *The Train Dogs*, a poem it later featured on its cover. Walter McRaye, who managed Pauline's business affairs for the last fourteen years of her life, says she made less than five hundred dollars from her poetry during her lifetime. She did much better financially from her short stories and other prose works. Her first magazine article, on Indian medicine-men, was sold to the *Dominion Illustrated* in 1892, and thereafter Miss Johnson produced a steady stream of articles, nature sketches and short stories for such publications as *Harper's Weekly*, *Saturday Night*, the Toronto *Globe*, the *Canadian Magazine*, and various English publications. In 1906 Pauline sold her first boy's story to *The Boy's World*, and during the next several years wrote more than a score of stories for this magazine. One of them was called *The Shaganappi*, and this was the title under which a collection of these stories was published in 1913, after her death, by Briggs of Toronto, which also published another collection of her prose work in the same year under the title *The Mocassin Maker*.

It may be wondered if Pauline would not have been better off financially, as well as professionally, if she had concentrated on producing and selling more work. After she settled in Vancouver in 1909 she gave every indication of being able to cope successfully with the problem of earning a living. However, it has to be remembered that by 1909 Pauline was better known than she was fifteen years earlier, and had less difficulty in placing her work. Moreover, in 1894, Pauline had pressing financial obligations towards her mother. It was, in fact, nagging poverty that made her embark on her recital tours that used up her time, and consumed her energies, during the next fifteen years. It must be remembered that travel in those days was not the fast and easy thing it is to-day. Pauline had more than her share of rough roads, spring-less buckboards, hard beds, unheated rooms and coarse food. Worst of all was the absence of opportunity for leisurely thought or creative work.

It is interesting to speculate in what way the story might have been different, both for Pauline and for Canadian lit-erature, if she had been able to find another solution to her money problems. One has only to compare her early work, as it appeared in *The White Wampum*, with her later work, as presented in *Canadian Born*, published in 1903, to realize that her tours were a handicap to the development of her genius. Apart from the deadening of the creative spirit in the tiring pressures and confusion of constant travelling, her platform appearances encouraged Pauline to write a great deal of shallow verse on contemporary topics which no doubt made good rousing recitations at the time but are far from being the stuff out of which lasting literature is made.

On the other hand, although Miss Johnson's platform appearances did little for her art, or for Canadian literature, they did make a contribution to Canada in a far different field. To appreciate this, we must try to visualize the Can-adian scene at the turn of the century. It was a Canada of vast distances, bridged only sketchily by the transcontinental railway system and their accompanying telegraph services. From Ontario to the Pacific coast, scores of settlements were putting down roots, many of them beyond the reach of the railway and therefore very remote from the rest of the country. Indeed many of these settlements were in closer contact, and in closer sympathy, with the adjoining United States, than they were with other parts of Canada. Miss Johnson swept into those remote communities like a vigorous and refreshing wind from civilization, bringing not only entertainment but a vision of Canada stretching from sea to sea. She preached the gospel of a united Canada at a time when the concept of Canada had still not encompassed the separate and rival concepts of Ontario, British Columbia, Nova Scotia, or even more limited regions. She brought word of a great new country stretching from the Atlantic to the Pacific at a time when the West was but a shapeless dream in the minds of most Canadians from Ontario to the Maritimes. And to the small new communities in the west and north she brought a sense of belonging to a great and growing nation.

At all times she expressed an unbounded confidence in the future of Canada, while many Canadians were still only hazily aware of the resources at their command. And in her own person she was tangible proof that Canada had a past that extended back beyond the arrival of the white man — a past, moreover, in which she proclaimed that all Canadians should take unqualified pride. In short, as William Arthur Deacon put it in the Toronto *Saturday Night*: "Canada means a little more because Pauline Johnson lived and wrote in it."

Pauline started her first comprehensive Canadian tour immediately on her return from London towards the end of 1894. Three years later she met Walter McRaye, a fellow entertainer from Merrickville, Ontario, fifteen years her junior, making his first professional tour. They joined forces for appearances in Winnipeg, Brandon and Portage la Prairie, Pauline as usual reciting her own poems and McRaye presenting the *habitant* verse of William Henry Drummond. These joint appearances were tremendously successful, presaging the close cooperation between Miss Johnson and McRaye in the years to come. But their partnership could not be continued at that time, as McRaye had to leave to carry out engagements in the United States, and Pauline had commitments in Western Canada.

The following year, 1898, turned out to be be a decisive one for Pauline. This was the year her mother died, a tragic blow for Pauline who had been very close to her mother, and now needlessly regretted the calls that had taken her so far from this beloved figure during the previous half-dozen years. This death, while freeing Pauline from any further financial obligations to her mother, also served to break her last ties with Brantford, and after she left the city later that year she never saw it again. Her father's house still lay empty and untended on the Reservation, but that she felt was the concern of her sister Evelyn, the only one of the Johnson family still living in Brantford. By this time the sisters were not on such terms as encouraged visiting. Her favourite brother Allen was working for the Canada Life Assurance Company in Toronto and living in Oakville. He was the only one of the family to marry, but did so late in life and did not have any children. Her older brother Beverly was working as cashier for the North American Life Insurance Company in Montreal. Later he was sent to the Philadelphia office of that company and was the first one of the family to die, suffering a heart attack one day in a street in Lancaster. His body was returned for burial in the grounds of the old Mohawk Chapel in Brantford where his parents and grandparents already lay.

For several months after the death of her mother, Pauline appeared to be undecided as to what course her future life should take. There was no longer the pressing financial need to continue with her strenuous schedule of platform appearances, and she was already beginning to express a desire to settle down behind a door of her own, where she could see the same landscape every time she looked through her own windows. But this was not to be. Before long she started out again, driven into an incredible unbroken ten-year series of tours by another event of 1898 which had an over-riding influence over her future life and work.

On January 26, 1898, the *Brantford Courier* carried a notice of the engagement of Emily Pauline Johnson to Charles Drayton of Toronto, Assistant Inspector of Western Loan and Savings Company of Winnipeg. Later, the *Courier* of July 30 carried this item under the photograph of Miss Johnson: "Countless friends and admirers of Brantford's talented authoress, Miss E. Pauline Johnson, will be sorry to learn that she is about to sever the ties which have hitherto tied her to this community. After her marriage takes place in Winnipeg, she will take up her permanent home in that prairie city. . ."

No date was mentioned for the marriage, which from the beginning had two strikes against it. In 1898, very few young men of respectable family, and Pauline would not consider any other as a marriage prospect, would be strong enough to resist family opposition to a marriage with an Indian. Furthermore, Pauline's way of life would be an obstacle to most middle-class mothers, who would be horrified at the idea of a son marrying an "actress." Actually, it has never been stated definitely why the marriage did not take place, but there is every indication that Pauline was terribly hurt.

Shortly after her death, her old friend, the poet Charles

Mair, wrote an appreciation in the *Canadian Magazine* in which he said that when he first met Pauline "she was absorbed in the fervour of an ill-fated engagement. Her strong, yet refined, features lighted up when she spoke of this with reticence, but with a transparent trustfulness as to its outcome. She had felt vividly. She had come, as she says in *Wavewon*: "To idolize the perfect world, to taste of love at last."

As to why her trust was misplaced, Pauline has left no record. But, as Mr Mair goes on to say: "The defeat of love runs like a grey thread through much of Miss Johnson's verse."

The wistful, renunciatory tone of Pauline's love lyrics was also commented on by Dr. John Logan in his *Highways of Canadian Literature*, published in 1924. After stating that "Pauline Johnson has yet to be equalled by other Canadian poets as a lyricist of the passion and pathos of romantic love", Dr. Logan goes on to say: "The tones of melancholy, of sadness, observed sometimes in Pauline Johnson's poetry were not all born of a mystical yearning for union with Nature. Sometimes they were the expression of a poignant sense of the defeat of romantic love."

This poignancy has given rise to some of Pauline's most memorable lines:

"*O, Love, thou wanderer from Paradise, dost thou not know*

How oft my lonely heart has cried to thee?

But Thou, and Sleep, and Peace, come not to me."

Or, in *The Prodigal*:

"*My heart forgot its God for love of you,*

And you forgot me, other loves to learn."

Whatever its cause, the break of her engagement was definite by the end of 1898, and early in the following year we find Pauline embarked on another tour of Canada. The tour opened in Ottawa under the patronage of the Governor General and Lady Minto, with Sir Wilfred and Lady Laurier and numerous other notables in the audience. Miss Johnson started this tour with Walter McRaye as her partner and manager — a relationship that ended only with her death.

A GREAT PUBLIC EVENT

During the next ten years, Miss Johnson and McRaye were almost constantly on the move. They crossed Canada many times from sea to sea, following not only the highways but also the byways.

"There is hardly a town or settlement in Canada that we did not visit," McRaye wrote later. "We gave the pioneer show in such places as Olds, Weyburn, Swift Current, Melville, Melfort and others. When we played in Saskatoon it was a village of three hundred souls. In many places ours was the first outside entertainment they had seen for many years, and the goodnatured people often rode fifty or sixty miles in order to hear us."

As an example of how they attracted people from a wide area, McRaye tells of the visit they made to Barville in British Columbia in 1903. The town had once been a thriving mining centre, but it had become a ghost town, with only about three hundred people remaining, all too old to try to start again elsewhere. Nevertheless Pauline and McRaye played to good houses. As McRaye reported: "Our house ran to five hundred and forty dollars the first night, and one hundred and eighty dollars the second."

Also in British Columbia that year, they ran into a by-election campaign at Lac La Hache in the Lillooet country. Just as they started their concert, in a large barn situated on the edge of a lake surrounded by high hills, the provincial premier, Richard MacBride and the attorney-general Charles Wilson drove up and wanted to know what was going on.

When they found out they decided to stay until the end of the concert, around 10:00 p.m., and then they harangued the crowd on political issues until midnight. Afterwards they all danced until dawn.

"It was a scene reminiscent of some western movie," McRaye recalled later, "with miners, ranchers, cowboys, half-breeds and Indians, dressed in riding chaps, overalls and various casual combinations, their ladies in fashions ranging from the bustle to puff sleeves. The Premier in an old tweed suit, a handkerchief around his neck, his youthful face surmounted with a shock of prematurely white hair which had earned him the nickname Handsome Dick, dancing with Pauline in a beautifully brocaded silk gown from London...."

In 1906 they went to England, where they opened a tour in London's great Steinway Hall. Concerning this, the *Morning Post* of July 17th, 1906, had this to say:

"An entertainment of an unusual kind was provided at the Steinway Hall last evening by Miss E. Pauline Johnson and Mr. Walter McRaye. Miss Johnson, who is descended from a former member of the Iroquois nation of Red Indians, recited, or rather enacted, a number of Indian stories of which she is author. These little pieces are powerfully descriptive and they gain considerably from the admirable manner in which they are interpreted. Miss Johnson has a dramatic manner, and she carried out her work with the aid of much picturesque, natural and remarkably effective gestures. . . . The audience showed every appreciation of the novel entertainment...."

It was on this second visit to London that Pauline met Chief Joe of the Capilano tribe of Squamish Indians, who was to have an important influence on her work. Chief Joe was one of three Pacific Coast chieftains who had gone to London on their own to protest to the King about a British

Columbia games act which they regarded as restricting their ancient fishing rights. They found London strange and bewildering, and were pleased and grateful to have a visit from Pauline who could talk their own language and could serve as a guide and a friend. On their return to British Columbia, after having been graciously received by King Edward VII, one of the memories they carried home was of the beautiful Mohawk poetess who was received everywhere in London as a great lady.

This was the beginning of a friendship that was to have valuable consequences for Pauline, after she had stopped her travels and settled down, never to tour again. But there were still several years of wandering to come before this happened, and another trip to London in 1907.

FINAL HOME AND LAST WORK

Pauline did not get around to regular creative writing again until she settled in Vancouver in 1909, ill and worn-out, although convinced in her own mind that she was only tired and in need of a good rest. During the next year, until Chief Joe died in 1910, she heard from his own lips some of the ancient legends of his people, which she started writing down for her readers. This was the first attempt to record the tribal mythology of the Pacific Coast Indians and, unlike later collectors of folk tales, Pauline felt free to embellish the simple legends with her Victorian literary accomplishments. The result is a group of stories of remarkable charm and lasting interest. Published under the collective title *Legends of Vancouver*, they are perhaps Miss Johnson's most substantial contribution to Canadian literature.

Concerning Chief Joe, Miss Johnson once described him as "rather a forceful character, and a strange and wonderful teller of tales. There was no use in asking him for anything.

❦ 32

One had to wait and be patient. Often he would come to visit me and, after sitting a while, depart without saying a word. But I never urged him, although he knew very well how I loved to hear his stories. My reward always came sooner or later when, suddenly, he would say 'You would like to know this' and then would follow a wondrous tale, full of strange wild poetry — the kind of folklore which soon will be heard no longer for the Indians are forgetting."

Fortunately, Miss Johnson was able to preserve some of these stories for posterity. The first of her Legends, *The Two Sisters*, was accepted by Lionel Makovski, editor of the weekly magazine section of the Vancouver *Province* and appeared on April 16, 1910. Thereafter they appeared with decreasing regularity until Pauline was too ill to do any more creative work. By the time she consulted a doctor, cancer had progressed too far to be operable, and all that could be done was to prescribe drugs to make the pain bearable. Before the end of 1911, the dosage of opiates was so great as to make impossible any but the fleetest flashes of creative work.

It was at this time that a group of friends in Vancouver, knowing that Pauline needed financial help but would be too proud to accept any, worked out a plot that not only brought her physical comfort during her last months but also a great deal of joy and satisfaction. They raised money to have a selection of her *Legends of Vancouver* published, but let Pauline think it was a straight business proposition, which of course it eventually became. The first two editions of 1,000 copies each were quickly sold, pushed by the Press Club, the Women's Canadian Club, the I.O.D.E. and other groups in Vancouver. When Walter McRaye started sending letters out to Pauline's friends all over Canada asking them to buy the book because of her illness and financial need, it was possible to dispose of a third edition of 10,000 copies at $2.00 each. The flood of cheques enabled Pauline to pay her own way right to the end, but possibly she was cheered even more by the numerous letters and expressions of affection that accompanied the cheques.

The first three editions were printed in Vancouver, but in 1912 the copyright was bought by McClelland and Stewart in Toronto who brought out a new edition of the Legends which was reprinted in 1961. By this time there was a growing demand for Pauline's verse. Her *White Wampum*, published eighteen years earlier, was now out of print, as was her later *Canadian Born*. The Musson Book Company of Toronto met the need by combining both of these volumes, adding a handful of as yet unpublished poems, and publishing them under the title *Flint and Feather*.

Pauline picked the title for her new volume, and explained her choice in an introductory note: "This collection I have named *Flint and Feather* because of the association of ideas. Flint suggests the Red Man's weapon of war; it is the arrow tip, the heart quality of mine own people. Let it, therefore, apply to those poems that touch upon Indian life and love. The lyrical verse herein is as 'A skyward-floating feather, sailing on summer air.' And yet that feather may be the eagle plume that crests the head of a warrior chief. So both flint and feather bear the hall-mark of my Mohawk blood."

Flint and Feather for many years was unfortunately labelled "the complete poems of E. Pauline Johnson," which it was not. The task of selection was left to a group of well-meaning ladies of the I.O.D.E. in Vancouver who quite reasonably shrank from making any selection at all. They simply lumped together all that had appeared in her two published volumes and added enough of her other published work to make up a volume of respectable size. They did not make use of any poems still in manuscript form. Some that they overlooked are included here among Miss Johnson's best work.

One of her Vancouver friends, Mrs. Garland Foster, who wrote a book about Pauline under the title *The Mohawk Princess*, once related that when the poems were being compiled some tender love lyrics were omitted as being "too personal". It was assumed they were left among Pauline's possessions which eventually passed into the care of her sister Evelyn. This may have been so—unfortunately, in view of the fact that Evelyn was definitely not a person to place literary value ahead of what she regarded as moral considerations. Certainly, none of Pauline's manuscript poems was found among Evelyn's papers after she died.

Walter McRaye has expressed his belief that Pauline's last year was a happy one for her, although she was in frequent pain and knew she was dying. The demand for her books brought her a realization that she would not be forgotten, that her work would live on. She was touched by the expressions of affection that poured in from all over Canada, and from her friends in England, and was gratified that she had the means to leave tokens of remembrance to scores of people in her will.

Pauline had always delighted in doing things for other people, in sharing such good fortune as came her way with those whose fortunes were low. Hector Charlesworth, in his book of personal reminiscences called *Candid Chronicles*, wrote: "I have met many literary women, but none with quite so interesting a personality as Miss Johnson. By nature she was the soul of generosity and her money, when she had it, literally ran through her fingers. On one occasion, before she was famous but had a few hundred dollars, she paid out every cent of it to save from prosecution a young bank clerk of her acquaintance who had been guilty of speculation. She did it too without letting him know. But his employer let the young man know who his benefactor was. In after years I asked her if the money had ever been repaid. 'No,' she said, 'but let's not talk of it,' and she immediately started talking about something else."

Walter McRaye, after touring with her for ten years, had a fund of stories about Pauline's good nature and concern for other people. One story tells of how the two of them, leaving Regina on an early morning train, met a harrassed woman with four small crying children. Pauline immediately took the youngest baby into her arms so that the woman could look after the others. The woman told them that her brother had just died and she was taking his children back to her small farm in Manitoba, where she had several children of her own. "We haven't much," she said, "but we'll get along somehow."

Miss Johnson never lost track of that family and frequently sent gifts to the baby, whom the woman called Pauline in honour of their benefactor. McRaye says that several years after Pauline's death he met a handsome young school teacher in Winnipeg who introduced herself as the baby of that train ride, and said that the family had always held Pauline's memory dear for her extraordinary kindness.

People who saw Pauline only across the footlights sometimes got a different impression of her personality. One story she was always fond of telling was that once after a recital in Medicine Hat she overheard a man say as he was leaving the concert hall: "She's a wild 'un, all right. Sure wouldn't want to have her as a wife."

In May, 1912, Pauline was admitted to a private hospital on Bute Street in Vancouver, where she could have constant medical attention and still be free to entertain her friends and come and go as freely as she was able. Her reaction to her disease was best expressed in her stirring poem, *Fight On*, written shortly after her doctor told her that she had only a few months left to live. During her last year she made fit-

❧ 36

ful efforts to do something she had long dreamed of doing
— to write a series of ballads taken from the folk-lore of the
Pacific Coast Indians, as related to her by Chief Joe. She
managed to complete only one of these, *The Ballad of Yaada.*
This, her last poem, was to have been printed in the Christmas 1912 number of *Saturday Night,* but unfortunately did
not appear until after Pauline had died. Another ballad was
started, *The Ballad of Laloo,* but Pauline never got beyond
the first few lines:

"*This is Laloo, Chief of the tribe whose feet*
Follow the murmuring Illecillewaet
As through the mighty Selkirk Range it strays
Singing and sighing down its waterways."

TRIBUTES TO A PRINCESS

Pauline died on March 7, 1913. Her
funeral three days later, on what would have been her fifty-
second birthday, became almost an occasion of national
mourning. Wreaths and condolences poured in from the
Governor-General, the Prime Minister and his cabinet, the
Royal Society of Canada, Sir Wilfrid and Lady Laurier, and
numerous literary and national organizations. Flags hung at
half-mast throughout Vancouver, and civic offices were closed
as the Mayor and Aldermen attended the service at Christ
Church, along with other leaders of civic and provincial life.
The I.O.D.E. was represented by Lady Tupper, who had
known Pauline when she was the literary lioness of the London season two decades earlier. The Pacific coast Indians were
represented by a large group of silent mourners, headed by
Chief atthias, the son of Chief Joe.

Pauline had expressed a wish to be cremated and her
ashes laid to rest in Stanley Park at a tree-shaded site over-
looking the sea where, during her long illness, she had
loved to sit and muse. As Stanley Park was military property

this wish could be granted only by the Department of National Defense. Final permission came from the Minister, Colonel Sam Hughes, at the intercession of the Governor-General. Thousands of ordinary citizens lined the route as the solemn procession wound its way from the church to Pauline's final, and most romantic, resting place. And all across the country, many other friends and admirers who were not able to be at the funeral, expressed their feelings of loss. In Montreal, William Douw Lighthall exclaimed: "How good she was. What a Princess in all respects, and how stately and generous as an intellectual celebrity. Her spirit lives among great trees. . . ."

In Toronto, Wilson MacDonald wrote an ode to her memory, containing these lines:

"A Princess, Poet, Woman, three in one,
    And fine in every measure of the three."

In Vancouver, her friend and editor, Lionel Makovski, wrote a moving tribute in *The Province*: "The inspiration of her genius was all Canadian, and all she wrote betrayed her love of the country which has passed from the rule of her fathers into the hands of aliens. . . . She was one of those great souls who would unwearyingly labour for her companions.... she loved life with a passionate intensity that was almost pathetic in its intensity. . ."

That was the theme of newspaper comment all across Canada on the day of her funeral, and even overseas where, reading of the ceremony and the numerous tributes, Theodore Watts-Dunton, whom Pauline had often called her literary father because he had encouraged her by praise of her early work, wrote: "This must have been the most picturesque and impressive funeral ever given any poet."

During her visits to London, Pauline had made a point of visiting Mr. Watts-Dunton and his friend the poet Algernon Swinburne, and from those few visits came the sincere tribute from Swinburne, when the news of her death reached London: "We can never forget Pauline."

At the time it seemed unlikely that her memory ever would fade. On the Sunday after her death, a moving memorial service was held in the little Mohawk Chapel on the Brantford Reservation where Pauline had often knelt as a child, in company with her mother and father, her brothers and sister. Later in the burial ground of the chapel, where lie her parents and grandparents, a massive boulder was placed, marked with an arrowhead and bearing these words:

E. Pauline Johnson
Mohawk Indian
Born March 10, 1861
at
Chiefswood
Six Nations Reserve
Died March 7, 1913
Interred in
Stanley Park
Vancouver B.C.

Nine years later, in 1922, a cairn was erected over her ashes in Stanley Park, dedicated "in memory of one whose life and writings were an uplift and a blessing to our nation."

It seems clear that most of those who mourned Miss Johnson's passing, and who paid sincere and warm tribute to her memory, regarded her as something other than a writer of poems, no matter how beautiful some of them were. To thousands of Canadians she was a vivid entertainer; a rare, warm and thrilling personality; a beautiful, generous woman; a stirring, dramatic monologuist; an aristocratic representative of the proud Mohawk nation, and a chronicler of Indian ways and legends.

Now that a new generation has emerged which has not come under the influence of her magnetic personality, it is possible to assess Miss Johnson solely as a writer, on the evidence of her existing work. Up to now it has not been possible to do that with any degree of fairness, as a great deal of her work has not been easily available to the public. Her two prose volumes, published in 1913, have long been out of print. Many of her best poems were to be found only in old magazines stacked away in libraries. Her only book that remained constantly on sale was *Flint and Feather* which, in spite of new concepts of poetry and the realization that much of the praise heaped upon her at her death was excessive, has long since achieved a greater sale than any other book of Canadian poetry.

Some years ago a scholarly society in Brantford, the Institute of Iroquoian Studies, pointed out that the time had come to take a fresh look at Miss Johnson and to reappraise her contributions to Canada. It was largely due to the work of this society, and particularly to one of its members, Richard Pilant, that a commemorative postage stamp was issued in 1961, honouring Pauline on the one hundredth anniversary of her birth. The institute also urged that Miss Johnson's best work be gathered together and published in a convenient volume, and it persuaded the Six Nations Council on the Brantford reservation to restore and preserve 'Chiefswood', Miss Johnson's birthplace.

This fine old residence, set in a spacious park about fourteen miles from Brantford, is open to the public during the summer months as a fine example of colonial architecture and Victorian living. It is furnished in the style of 1870, and one can easily imagine Pauline as a child living happily in these surroundings. Some of the furniture belonged to the Johnsons, and the rest has been carefully selected as harmonizing both in period and in style. Even the wallpaper and drapes are genuinely in keeping with the 1870 period and the taste of Chief Johnson and his English bride. Pauline's bedroom is intact as it was when she was a child, with its windows overlooking the Grand River, and the writing table where Pauline wrote her first experimental verses and stories.

Other rooms of the house contain family portraits, the remnants of the once-fine Johnson library, and many interesting souvenirs of Pauline. For example, there is a letter, dated March 4, 1891, expressing in the cobweb-fine script of the aging John Greenleaf Whittier appreciation of Pauline's first Indian poems. "It is fitting," wrote the Quaker poet, "that one of their race should sing the songs of the Mohawk and the Iroquois in the English tongue. There is a splendid opportunity before thee. And I am very glad to see the fine and thoughtful face of the young poet, for which I truly thank thee."

There are also many Pauline Johnson souvenirs in the Brant Historical Museum in Brantford, which has added considerably to its collection in recent years as a result of the revival of interest in Pauline which has persuaded people who owned mementoes in any way connected with her to hand them over to the Museum's care. There is also a Pauline Johnson corner of the Vancouver Museum, where her Indian costume, as she wore it during her recital appearances, is on display. A much more important collection is at McMaster University in Hamilton, which received a great deal of Pauline Johnson material under the wills of Pauline's sister, Evelyn, and Pauline's friend and co-worker Walter McRaye.

Unfortunately both Evelyn Johnson and Walter McRaye edited the material before their deaths. One report says that McRaye burned a great many of Pauline's personal letters and diaries which had been left in his possession. The result is that many of the questions surrounding Pauline's life remain unanswered.

The eminent geologist Dr Gilbert Monture, who was born on the Brantford Reservation and had family connections with the Johnsons, tells how he visited McRaye in 1947, after the publication of his two books of reminiscences about Pauline, *Town Hall Tonight* and *Pauline Johnson and Her Friends*. Dr Monture says that in the hope of getting some information that might give a clue to Pauline's intriguing personality, he made every effort to break down his inhibitions. Finally, he says, towards the close of the evening, McRaye slapped Dr Monture on the shoulder, and said: "I know what you are after, Doctor, but you will never hear any word pass my lips that would in anyway affect the reputation of our dear and gracious Pauline".

This attitude on the part of Pauline's friends presents a formidable challenge to Pauline's biographers. It is to be hoped that the publication of this collection of some of the best prose and poetry of Pauline Johnson will encourage some future, patient, chronicler to probe into the mysteries that still surround the life of this fascinating personality who was the sole poetic voice in English of the Indian people of Canada.

❦ POEMS

❧ ON THE DEDICATION OF A MEMORIAL TO JOSEPH BRANT

Young Canada with mighty force sweeps on
To gain in power and strength before the dawn
That brings another era, when the sun
Shall rise again, but sadly shine upon
Her Indian graves and Indian memories.
For as the carmine in the twilight skies
Will fade as night comes on, as fades the race
That unto Might and doubtful Right gives place.
And as white clouds float hurriedly and high
Across the crimson of a sunset sky
Altho' their depths are foamy as the snow
Their beauty lies in their vermillion glow.
So, Canada, thy plumes were hardly won
Without allegiance from thy Indian son.
Thy glories, like the cloud, enhance their charm
With red reflections from the Mohawk's arm.
Then meet we as one common brotherhood
In peace and love, with purpose understood
To lift a lasting tribute to the name
Of Brant, who linked his own with Britain's fame.
Who bade his people leave their Valley Home
Where nature in her fairest aspects shone,
Where rolls the Mohawk River and the land
is blest with every good from Heaven's hand,
To sweep the tide of home affections back
And love the land where waves the Union Jack.

What tho' that home no longer ours? Today
The Six Red Nations have their Canada.
And rest we here, no cause for us to rise
To seek protection under other skies.
Encircling us an arm both true and brave
Extends from far across the great salt wave.
Tho' but a woman's arm, 'tis firm, and strong
Enough to guard us from all fear of wrong,
An arm on which all British subjects lean —
The loving hand of England's noble Queen.
Chiefswood

October 8th, 1886   TEKAHIONWAKE

So still the tranquil air,
One scarcely notes the falling of a leaf—
But deeper quiet wraps the dusky Chief
Whose ashes slumber there.

Sweet Indian Summer sleeps—
Trusting a foreign and a paler race
To give her gifted son an honoured place
Where Death his vigil keeps.

Before that slumber fell,
Those ashes in their eloquence had stirred
The stubborn hearts, whose heirs to-day conferred
A Christian burial.

Through war's o'er-clouded skies
His higher flush of oratory 'woke,
And factious schemes succumbed whene'er he spoke
To bid his people rise.

The keenest flint or stone
That barbed the warrior's arrow in its flight
Could not out-reach the limit of his might
That he attained alone.

Early he learned to speak,
With thought so vast, and liberal, and strong,
He blessed the little good and passed the wrong
Embodied in the weak.

The world has often seen
His master mind pulse with the dying day
That sends his waning nation to decay
Where none can intervene.

And few to-day remain:
But copper-tinted face, and smoldering fire
Of wilder life, were left me by my sire
To be my proudest claim.

And so ere Indian Summer sweetly sleeps
She beckons me where old Niagara leaps;
Superbly she extends her greeting hand,
And, smiling, speaks to her adopted land,
Saying: 'O rising nation of the West
That occupy my lands so richly blest;
O free unfettered people who have come
And made America young rightful home —
Forgive the wrongs my children did to you,
And we, the red-skins, will forgive you too.
Today has seen your noblest action done —
The honoured re-intombment of my son."

(Buffalo, New York, October 1884)

🌷 48

I am Ojistoh, I am she, the wife
Of him whose name breathes bravery and life
And courage to the tribe that calls him chief.
I am Ojistoh, his white star, and he
Island, and lake, and sky — and soul to me.

Ah! but they hated him, those Huron braves,
Him who had flung their warriors into graves,
Him who had crushed them underneath his heel,
Whose arm was iron, and whose heart was steel
To all — save me, Ojistoh, chosen wife
Of my great Mohawk, white star of his life.

Ah! but they hated him, and councilled long
With subtle witchcraft how to work him wrong;
How to avenge their dead, and strike him where
His pride was highest, and his fame most fair.
Their hearts grew weak as women at his name:
They dared no war-path since my Mohawk came
With ashen bow, and flinten arrow-head
To pierce their craven bodies; but their dead
Must be avenged. Avenged? They dared not walk
In day and meet his deadly tomahawk;
They dared not face his fearless scalping knife;
So — Niyoh — then they thought of me, his wife.

O! evil, evil face of them they sent
With evil Huron speech: "Would I consent
To take of wealth? be queen of all their tribe?
Have wampum ermine?" Back I flung the bribe
Into their teeth, and said, "While I have life
Know this — Ojistoh is the Mohawk's wife."

Wah! how we struggled! But their arms were strong.
They flung me on their pony's back, with thong
Round ankle, wrist, and shoulder. Then upleapt
The one I hated most: his eye he swept
Over my misery, and sneering said,
"Thus, fair Ojistoh, we avenge our dead."

And we two rode, rode as a sea wind-chased,
I, bound with buckskin to his hated waist,
He, sneering, laughing, jeering, while he lashed
The horse to foam, as on and on we dashed.
Plunging through creek and river, bush and trail,
On, on we galloped like a northern gale.
At last, his distant Huron fires aflame
We saw, and nearer, nearer still we came.

I, bound behind him in the captive's place,
Scarcely could see the outline of his face.
I smiled, and laid my cheek against his back:
"Loose thou my hands," I said. "This pace let slack.
Forget we now that thou and I are foes.
I like thee well, and wish to clasp thee close;
I like the courage of thine eye and brow;
I LIKE THEE BETTER THAN MY MOHAWK NOW."

He cut the cords; we ceased our maddened haste
I wound my arms about his tawny waist;
My hand crept up the buckskin of his belt;
His knife hilt in my burning palm I felt;
One hand caressed his cheek, the other drew
The weapon softly — "I love you, love you,"
I whispered, "love you as my life."
And — buried in his back his scalping knife.

Ha! how I rode, rode as a sea wind-chased,
Mad with sudden freedom, mad with haste,
Back to my Mohawk and my home. I lashed
That horse to foam, as on and on I dashed.
Plunging thro' creek and river, bush and trail,
On, on I galloped like a northern gale.
And then my distant Mohawk's fires aflame
I saw, as nearer, nearer still I came,
My hands all wet, stained with a life's red dye,
But pure my soul, pure as those stars on high —
"My Mohawk's pure white star, Ojistoh, still am I."

Captive! Is there a hell to him like this?
A taunt more galling than the Huron's hiss?
He — proud and scornful, he — who laughed at law,
He — scion of the deadly Iroquois,
He — the bloodthirsty, he — the Mohawk chief,
He — who despises pain and sneers at grief,
Here in the hated Huron's vicious clutch,
That even captive he disdains to touch!

Captive! But NEVER conquered; Mohawk brave
Stoops not to be to ANY man a slave;
Least, to the puny tribe his soul abhors,
The tribe whose wigwams sprinkles Simcoe's shores.
With scowling brow he stands and courage high,
Watching with haughty and defiant eye
His captors, as they council o'er his fate,
Or strive his boldness to intimidate.
Then fling they unto him the choice;

"Wilt thou
Walk o'er the bed of fire that waits thee now —
Walk with uncovered feet upon the coals,
Until thou reach the ghostly Land of Souls,
And, with thy Mohawk death-song please our ear?
OR WILT THOU WITH THE WOMEN REST THEE
    HERE?"

His eyes flashed like an eagle's, and his hands
Clench at the insult. Like a god he stands.
"Prepare the fire!" he scornfully demands.
He knoweth not that this same jeering band
Will bite the dust — will lick the Mohawk's hand;
Will kneel and cower at the Mohawk's feet;
Will shrink when Mohawk war drums wildly beat.

His death will be avenged with hideous hate
By Iroquois, swift to annihilate
His vile detested captors, that now flaunt
Their war clubs in his face with sneer and taunt,
Not thinking, soon that reeking, red, and raw,
Their scalps will deck the belts of Iroquois.

The path of coals outstretches, white with heat,
A forest fir's length — ready for his feet.
Unflinching as a rock he steps along
The burning mass, and sings his wild war song;
Sings, as he sang when once he used to roam
Throughout the forests of his southern home,
Where, down the Genesee, the water roars,
Where gentle Mohawk purls between its shores,
Songs, that of exploit and of prowess tell;
Songs of the Iroquois invincible.

Up the long trail of fire he boasting goes,
Dancing a war dance to defy his foes.
His flesh is scorched, his muscles burn and shrink,
But still he dances to death's awful brink.
The eagle plume that crests his haughty head
Will NEVER droop until his heart be dead.
Slower and slower yet his footstep swings,
Wilder and wilder still his death-song rings,
Fiercer and fiercer thro' the forest bounds
His voice that leaps to Happier Hunting Grounds.
One savage yell —
                    Then loyal to his race,
He bends to death — but NEVER to disgrace.

There's a spirit on the river, there's a ghost upon
                the shore,
They are chanting, they are singing through the
                starlight evermore,
As they steal amid the silence,
       And the shadows of the shore.

You can hear them when the Northern candles light
                the Northern sky,
Those pale, uncertain candle flames, that shiver,
                dart and die,
Those dead men's icy finger tips,
       Athwart the Northern sky.

You can hear the ringing war-cry of a long-for-
                gotten brave
Echo through the midnight forest, echo o'er the
                midnight wave,
And the Northern lanterns tremble
       At the war-cry of that brave.

And you hear a voice responding, but in soft and
                tender song;
It is Dawendine's spirit singing, singing all night
                long;
And the whisper of the night wind
       Bears afar her Spirit song.

And the wailing pine trees murmur with their voice
    attuned to hers,
Murmur when they 'rouse from slumber as the night
    wind through them stirs,
And you listen to their legend,
   And their voices blend with hers.

There was feud and there was bloodshed near the
    river by the hill;
And Dawendine listened, while her very heart stood
    still:
Would her kinsman or her lover
   Be the victim by the hill?

Who would be the great unconquered? who come
    boasting how he dealt
Death? and show his rival's scalplock fresh and
    bleeding at his belt.
Who would say, "O Dawendine!
   Look upon the death I dealt?"

And she listens, listens, listens — till a war-cry
    rends the night,
Cry of her victorious lover, monarch he of all the
    height;
And his triumph wakes the horrors,
   Kills the silence of the night.

❧ 56

Heart of her! it throbs so madly, then lies freezing
            in her breast,
For the icy hand of death has chilled the brother
            she loved best;
And her lover dealt the death-blow;
      And her heart dies in her breast.

And she hears her mother saying, "Take thy belt of
            wampum white;
Go unto yon evil savage while he glories
            on the height;
Sing and sue for peace between us:
      At his feet lay wampum white.

"Lest thy kinsmen all may perish, all thy brothers
            and thy sire
Fall before his mighty hatred as the forest
            falls to fire;
Take thy wampum pale and peaceful,
      Save thy brothers, save thy sire."

And the girl arises softly, softly slips toward
            the shore;
Loves she well the murdered brother, loves his
            hated foeman more,
Loves, and longs to give the wampum;
      And she meets him on the shore.

"Peace," she sings, "O mighty victor, Peace! I
          bring thee wampum white.
Sheathe thy knife whose blade has tasted my young
          kinsman's blood to-night
Ere it drink to slake its thirsting,
          I have brought thee wampum white."

Answers he, "O Dawendine! I will let thy
          kinsmen be,
I accept thy belt of wampum; but my hate
          demands for me
That they give their fairest treasure,
          Ere I let thy kinsmen be.

"Dawendine, for thy singing, for thy suing, war
          shall cease;
For thy name, which speaks of dawning, THOU shalt
          be the dawn of peace;
For thine eyes whose purple shadows tell of dawn,
          My hate shall cease.

"Dawendine, Child of Dawning, hateful are thy
          kin to me;
Red my fingers with their heart blood, but my
          heart is red for thee:
Dawendine, Child of Dawning,
          Wilt thou fail or follow me?"

And her kinsmen still are waiting her returning from
the night,
Waiting, waiting for her coming with her belt of
Wampum white;
But forgetting all, she follows,
Where he leads through day or night.

There's a spirit on the river, there's a ghost upon
the shore,
And they sing of love and loving through the star-
light evermore,
As they steal amid the silence,
And the shadows of the shore.

My Forest Brave, my Red-skin love, farewell;
We may not meet to-morrow; who can tell
What mighty ills befall our little band,
Or what you'll suffer from the white man's hand?
Here is your knife! I thought 'twas sheathed for aye.
No roaming bison calls for it to-day;
No hide of prairie cattle will it maim;
The plains are bare, it seeks a nobler game:
'Twill drink the life-blood of a soldier host.
Go; rise and strike, no matter what the cost.
Yet stay. Revolt not at the Union Jack,
Nor raise Thy hand against this stripling pack
Of white-faced warriors, marching West to quell
Our fallen tribe that rises to rebel.
They all are young and beautiful and good;
Curse to the war that drinks their harmless blood.
Curse to the fate that brought them from the East
To be our chiefs — to make our nation least
That breathes the air of this vast continent.
Still their new rule and council is well meant.
They but forget we Indians owned the land
From ocean unto ocean; that they stand
Upon a soil that centuries agone
Was our sole kingdom and our right alone.
They never think how they would feel to-day,
If some great nation came from far away,

Wresting their country from their hapless braves,
Giving what they gave us — but wars and graves.
Then go and strike for liberty and life,
And bring back honour to your Indian wife.
Your wife? Ah, what of that, who cares for me?
Who pities my poor love and agony?
What white-robed priest prays for your safety here,
As prayer is said for every volunteer
That swells the ranks that Canada sends out?
Who prays for vict'ry for the Indian scout?
Who prays for our poor nation lying low?
None — therefore take your tomahawk and go.
My heart may break and burn into its core,
But I am strong to bid you go to war.
Yet stay, my heart is not the only one
That grieves the loss of husband and of son;
Think of the mothers o'er the inland seas;
Think of the pale-faced maiden on her knees;
One pleads her God to guard some sweet-faced child
That marches on toward the North-West wild.
The other prays to shield her love from harm,
To strengthen his young, proud uplifted arm.
Ah, how her white face quivers thus to think
YOUR tomahawk his life's best blood will drink.
She never thinks of my wild aching breast,

Nor prays for your dark face and eagle crest
Endangered by a thousand rifle balls,
My heart the target if my warrior falls.
O! coward self I hesitate no more;
Go forth, and win the glories of the war.
Go forth, nor bend to greed of white men's hands,
By right, by birth we Indians own these lands,
Though starved, crushed, plundered, lies our nation low...
Perhaps the white man's God has willed it so.

Hard by the Indian lodges, where the bush
    Breaks in a clearing, through ill-fashioned fields,
She comes to labour, when the first still hush
    Of autumn follows large and recent yields.

Age in her fingers, hunger in her face,
    Her shoulders stooped with weight of work and years,
But rich in tawny colouring of her race,
    She comes a-field to strip the purple ears.

And all her thoughts are with the days gone by,
    Ere might's injustice banished from their lands
Her people, that to-day unheeded lie,
    Like the dead husks that rustle through her hands.

Little brown baby-bird, lapped in your nest,
                    Wrapped in your nest,
                    Strapped in your nest,
Your straight little cradle-board rocks you to rest;
                    Its hands are your nest;
                    Its bands are your nest;
It swings from the down-bending branch of the oak;
You watch the camp flame, and the curling grey smoke;
But, oh, for your pretty black eyes sleep is best,—
Little brown baby of mine, go to rest.

Little brown baby-bird swinging to sleep,
                    Winging to sleep,
                    Singing to sleep,
Your wonder-black eyes that so wide open keep,
                    Shielding their sleep,
                    Unyielding to sleep,
The heron is homing, the plover is still,
The night-owl calls from his haunt on the hill,
Afar the fox barks, afar the stars peep,—
Little brown baby of mine, go to sleep.

Plains, plains, and the prairie land which the
                    sunlight floods and fills,
To the north the open country, southward the
                    Cypress Hills;

Never a bit of woodland, never a rill that flows,
Only a stretch of cactus beds, and the wild, sweet
                    prairie rose;

Never a habitation, save where in the far south-west
A solitary tepee lifts its solitary crest,
Where Neykia in the doorway, crouched in the red
                    sunshine,
Broiders her buckskin mantle with the quills of
                    the porcupine.

Neykia, the Sioux chief's daughter, she with the
                    foot that flies,
She with the hair of midnight and the wondrous
                    midnight eyes,
She with the deft brown fingers, she with the soft,
                    slow smile,
She with the voice of velvet and the thoughts that
                    dream the while, —
"Whence come the vague to-morrows? Where
                    do the yesters fly?
What is beyond the border of the prairie
                    and the sky?

Does the maid in the Land of Morning sit in the
                red sunshine,
Broidering her buckskin mantle with the quills of
                the porcupine?"

So Neykia, in the westland, wonders and works
                away,
Far from the fret and folly of the "Land of Waking
                Day."

And many the pale-faced trader who stops at the
                tepee door
For a smile from the sweet, shy worker, and a sigh
                when the hour is o'er.

For they know of a young red hunter who often-
                times has stayed
To rest and smoke with her father, tho' his eyes
                were on the maid;

And the moons will not be many ere she in the red
                sunshine
Will broider his buckskin mantle with the quills
                of the porcupine.

He needs must leave the trapping and the chase,
        For mating game his arrows ne'er despoil,
And from the hunter's heaven turn his face,
        To wring some promise from the dormant soil.

He needs must leave the lodge that wintered him,
        The enervating fires, the blanket bed —
The women's dulcet voices, for the grim
        Realities of labouring for bread.

So goes he forth beneath the planter's moon
        With sack of seed that pledges large increase,
His simple pagan faith knows night and noon,
        Heat, cold, seedtime and harvest shall not cease.

And yielding to his needs, this honest sod,
        Brown as the hand that tills it, moist with rain,
Teeming with ripe fulfilment, true as God,
        With fostering richness, mothers every grain.

The sky-line melts from russet into blue,
Unbroken the horizon, saving where
A wreath of smoke curls up the far, thin air,
And points the distant lodges of the Sioux.

Etched where the lands and cloudlands touch and die
A solitary Indian tepee stands,
The only habitation of these lands.
That roll their magnitude from sky to sky.

The tent poles lift and loom in thin relief,
The upward floating smoke ascends between,
And near the open doorway, gaunt and lean,
And shadow-like, there stands an Indian Chief.

With eyes that lost their lustre long ago,
With visage fixed and stern as fate's decree,
He looks towards the empty west, to see
The never-coming herd of buffalo.

Only the bones that bleach upon the plains,
Only the fleshless skeletons that lie
In ghastly nakedness and silence, cry
Out mutely that naught else to him remains.

Into the rose gold westland, its yellow prairies roll,
World of the bison's freedom, home of the Indian's soul.
Roll out, O seas! in sunlight bathed,
Your plains wind-tossed, and grass enswathed.

Farther than vision ranges, farther than eagles fly,
Stretches the land of beauty, arches the perfect sky,
Hemm'd through the purple mists afar
By peaks that gleam like star on star.

Fringing the prairie billows, fretting horizon's line,
Darkly green are slumb'ring wildernesses of pine,
Sleeping until the zephyrs throng
To kiss their silence into song.

Whispers freighted with odour swinging into the air,
Russet needles as censers swing to an altar, where
The angels' songs are less divine
Than duo sung twixt breeze and pine.

Laughing into the forest, dimples a mountain stream,
Pure as the airs above it, soft as a summer dream,
O! Lethean spring thou'rt only found
Within this ideal hunting ground.

Surely the great Hereafter cannot be more than this,
Surely we'll see that country after Time's farewell kiss.
Who would his lovely faith condole?
Who envies not the Red-skin's soul?

Sailing into the cloud land, sailing into the sun,
Into the crimson portals ajar when life is done?
O! dear dead race, my spirit too
Would fain sail westward unto you.

I am the one who loved her as my life,
      Had watched her grow to sweet young womanhood;
Won the dear privilege to call her wife,
      And found the world, because of her, was good.
I am the one who heard the spirit voice,
      Of which the paleface settlers love to tell;
From whose strange story they have made their choice
      Of naming this fair valley the "Qu'Appelle."

She had said fondly in my eager ear —
      "When Indian summer smiles with dusky lip,
Come to the lakes, I will be first to hear
      The welcome music of thy paddle dip.
I will be first to lay in thine my hand,
      To whisper words of greeting on the shore;
And when thou would'st return to thine own land,
      I'll go with thee, thy wife for evermore."

Not yet a leaf had fallen, not a tone
      Of frost upon the plain ere I set forth,
Impatient to possess her as my own —
      This queen of all the women of the North.
I rested not at even or at dawn,
      But journeyed all the dark and daylight through —
Until I reached the Lakes, and, hurrying on,
      I launched upon their bosom my canoe.

Of sleep or hunger then I took no heed,
　　But hastened o'er their leagues of waterways;
But my hot heart outstripped my paddle's speed
　　And waited not for distance or for days,
But flew before me swifter than the blade
　　Of magic paddle ever cleaved the Lake,
Eager to lay its love before the maid,
　　And watch the lovelight in her eyes awake.

So the long days went slowly drifting past;
　　It seemed that half my life must intervene
Before the morrow, when I said at last —
　　"One more day's journey and I win my queen!"
I rested then, and, drifting, dreamed the more
　　Of all the happiness I was to claim, —
When suddenly from out the shadowed shore,
　　I heard a voice speak tenderly my name.

"Who calls?" I answered; no reply; and long
　　I stilled my paddle blade and listened. Then
Above the night wind's melancholy song
　　I heard distinctly that strange voice again —
A woman's voice, that through the twilight came
　　Like to a soul unborn — a song unsung.

I leaned and listened — yes, she spoke my name,
  And then I answered in the quaint French tongue,
"Qu'Appelle? Qu'Appelle?" No answer, and the night
  Seemed stiller for the sound, till round me fell
The far-off echoes from the far-off height —
  "Qu'Appelle?" my voice came back, "Qu'Appelle?
    Qu'Appelle?"
This — and no more; I called aloud until
  I shuddered as the gloom of night increased,
And, like a pallid spectre wan and chill,
  The moon arose in silence in the east.

I dare not linger on the moment when
  My boat I beached beside her tepee door;
I heard the wail of women and of men, —
  I saw the death-fires lighted on the shore
No language tells the torture or the pain,
  The bitterness that flooded all my life, —
When I was led to look on her again,
  That queen of women pledged to be my wife.
To look upon the beauty of her face,
  The still closed eyes, the lips that knew no breath;
To look, to learn, — to realize my place
  Had been usurped by my one rival — Death.
A storm of wrecking sorrow beat and broke
  About my heart, and life shut out its light
Till through my anguish some one gently spoke,
  And said, "Twice did she call for thee last night."

❦ 73

"False," they said, "thy Pale-face lover, from the
land of waking morn;
Rise and wed thy Redskin wooer, nobler warrior
ne'er was born;
Cease thy watching, cease thy dreaming,
Show the white thine Indian scorn."

Thus they taunted her, declaring, "He remembers
naught of thee:
Likely some white maid he wooeth, far beyond the
inland sea."
But she answered ever kindly,
"He will come again to me,"

Till the dusk of Indian summer crept athwart the
western skies;
But a deeper dusk was burning in her dark and
dreaming eyes,
As she scanned the rolling prairie,
Where the foothills fall, and rise.

Till the autumn came and vanished, till the season
of the rains,
Till the western world lay fettered in midwinter's
crystal chains,
Still she listened for his coming,
Still she watched the distant plains.

Then a night with nor'land tempest, nor'land snows
                a-swirling fast,
Out upon the pathless prairie came the Pale-face
                through the blast,
Calling, calling, "Yakonwita,
      I am coming, love, at last."

Hovered night above, about him, dark its wings and
                cold and dread;
Never unto trail or tepee were his straying
                footsteps led;
Till benumbed, he sank, and pillowed
      On the drifting snows his head,

Saying, "O! my Yakonwita call me, call me,
                be my guide
To the lodge beyond the prairie — for I vowed
                'ere winter died
I would come again, beloved;
      I would claim my Indian bride."

"Yakonwita, Yakonwita!" Oh, the dreariness
                that strains
Through the voice that calling, quivers, till
                a whisper but remains,
"Yakonwita, Yakonwita,
      I am lost upon the plains."

❧ 75

But the Silent Spirit hushed him, lulled him
                as he cried anew;
"Save me, save me! O! beloved, I am Pale but
                I am true.
Yakonwita, Yakonwita,
       I am dying, love, for you."

Leagues afar, across the prairie, she had risen
              from her bed,
Roused her kinsmen from their slumber: "He has
              come to-night," she said.
"I can hear him calling, calling;
       But his voice is as the dead.

"Listen!" and they sat all silent, while the
              tempest louder grew,
And a spirit-voice called faintly, "I am dying, love,
              for you."
Then they wailed, "O! Yakonwita
       He was Pale, but he was true."

Wrapped she then her ermine round her, stepped
              without the tepee door,
Saying, "I must follow, follow, though he call
              for evermore,
Yakonwita, Yakonwita;"
       And they never saw her more.

Late at night, say Indian hunters, when the
starlight clouds or wanes,
Far away they see a maiden, misty as the autumn
rains,
Guiding with her lamp of moonlight
Hunters lost upon the plains.

They were coming across the prairie, they were
        galloping hard and fast;
For the eyes of those desperate riders had sighted
        their man at last —
Sighted him off to Eastward, where the Cree
        encampment lay,
Where the cotton woods fringed the river, miles
        and miles away.
Mistake him? Never! Mistake him? the famous
        Eagle Chief!
That terror to all the settlers, that desperate
        Cattle Thief —
That monstrous, fearless Indian, who lorded it
        over the plain,
Who thieved and raided, and scouted, who rode
        like a hurricane!
But they've tracked him across the prairie; they've
        followed him hard and fast;
For those desperate English settlers have sighted
        their man at last.

Up they wheeled to the tepees, all their British
        blood aflame,
Bent on bullets and bloodshed, bent on bringing
        down their game;
But they searched in vain for the Cattle Thief: that
        lion had left his lair,

And they cursed like a troop of demons — for the
women alone were there.
"The sneaking Indian coward," they hissed; "he
hides while yet he can;
He'll come in the night for cattle, but he's scared
to face a MAN."
"Never!" and up from the cotton woods rang the
voice of Eagle Chief;
And right out into the open stepped, unarmed, the
Cattle Thief.
Was that the game they had coveted? Scarce fifty
years had rolled
Over that fleshless, hungry frame, starved to the
bone and old;
Over that wrinkled, tawny skin, unfed by the
warmth of blood.
Over those hungry, hollow eyes that glared for the
sight of food.

He turned, like a hunted lion: "I know not fear,"
said he;
And the words outleapt from his shrunken lips in
the language of the Cree.
"I'll fight you, white-skins, one by one, till I kill
you ALL," he said;
But the threat was scarcely uttered, ere a dozen
balls of lead

Whizzed through the air about him like a shower
of metal rain,
And the gaunt old Indian Cattle Thief dropped
dead on the open plain.
And that band of cursing settlers gave one
triumphant yell,
And rushed like a pack of demons on the body that
writhed and fell.
"Cut the fiend up into inches, throw his carcass on
the plain;
Let the wolves eat the cursed Indian, he'd have
treated us the same."
A dozen hands responded, a dozen knives gleamed
high,
But the first stroke was arrested by a woman's
strange, wild cry.
And out into the open, with a courage past
belief,
She dashed, and spread her blanket o'er the corpse
of the Cattle Thief;
And the word outleapt from her shrunken lips in
the language of the Cree,
"If you mean to touch that body, you must cut
your way through ME."
And that band of cursing settlers dropped
backward one by one,

For they knew that an Indian woman roused, was
a woman to let alone.
And then she raved in a frenzy that they scarcely
understood,
Raved of the wrongs she had suffered since her
earliest babyhood:
"Stand back, stand back, you white-skins, touch
that dead man to your shame;
You have stolen my father's spirit, but his body I
only claim.
You have killed him, but you shall not dare to
touch him now he's dead.
You have cursed, and called him a Cattle Thief,
though you robbed him first of bread —
Robbed him and robbed my people — look there,
at that shrunken face,
Starved with a hollow hunger, we owe to you
and your race.
What have you left to us of land, what have you
left of game,
What have you brought but evil, and curses since
you came?
How have you paid us for our game? how paid us
for our land?
By a BOOK, to save our souls from the sins YOU
brought in your other hand.

❦ 81

Go back with your new religion, we never have
        understood
Your robbing an Indian's BODY, and mocking his
        SOUL with food.
Go back with your new religion, and find — if find
        you can —
The HONEST man you have ever made from out a
        STARVING man.
You say your cattle are not ours, your meat is not
        our meat;
When YOU pay for the land you live in, WE'LL pay
        for the meat we eat.
Give back our land and our country, give back our
        herds of game;
Give back the furs and the forests that were ours
        before you came;
Give back the peace and the plenty. Then come
        with your new belief,
And blame, if you dare, the hunger that DROVE him
        to be a thief."

"Yes, sir, it's quite a story, though you won't
         believe it's true,
But such things happened often when I lived
         beyond the Soo."
And the trapper tilted back his chair and filled
         his pipe anew.

"I ain't thought of it neither fer this many 'n
         many a day,
Although it used to haunt me in the years that's
         slid away;
The years I spent a-trappin' for the good old
         Hudson's Bay.

"Wild? You bet, 'twas wild then, an' few an' far
         between
The squatters' shacks, for whites was scarce as furs
         when things is green,
An' only reds an' Hudson's men was all the folk
         I seen.

"No. Them old Indyans ain't so bad, not if you
         treat 'em square.
Why, I lived in amongst 'em all the winters I was
         there,
An' I never lost a copper, an' I never
         lost a hair.

"But I'd have lost my life the time that you've
heard tell about;
I don't think I'd be settin' here, but dead beyond
a doubt
If that there Indyan 'Wolverine' jest hadn't helped
me out.

" 'Twas freshet time, 'way back, as long as sixty-
six or eight,
An' I was coming to the Post that year a kind
of late,
For beaver had been plentiful, and trappin' had
been great.

"One day I had been settin' traps along a bit of
wood,
An' night was catchin' up to me jest faster 'an it
should,
When all at once I heard a sound that curdled up
my blood.

"It was the howl of famished wolves — I didn't
stop to think
But jest lit out across for home as quick as you
could wink,
But when I reached the river's edge I brought up
at the brink.

"That mornin' I had crossed the stream straight
on a sheet of ice
An' now, God help me! There it was, churned up
an' cracked to dice,
The flood went boiling past — I stood like one shut
in a vice.

"No way ahead, no path aback, trapped like a rat
ashore,
With naught but death to follow, and with naught
but death afore;
The howl of hungry wolves aback — ahead, the
torrent's roar.

"An' then — a voice, an Indyan voice, that called
out clear and clean,
'Take Indyan's horse, I run like deer, wolf can't
catch Wolverine.'
I says, 'Thank Heaven.' There stood the chief I'd
nicknamed Wolverine.

"I leapt on that there horse, an' then jest like a
coward fled,
An' left that Indyan standin' there alone, as good
as dead,
With the wolves a-howlin' at his back, the swollen
stream ahead.

"I don't know how them Indyans dodge from
death the way they do,
You won't believe it, sir, but what I'm tellin' you
is true,
But that there chap was 'round next day as sound
as me or you.

"He came to get his horse, but not a cent he'd
take from me.
Yes, sir, you're right, the Indyans now ain't like
they used to be;
We've got 'em sharpened up a bit an' NOW they'll
take a fee.

"No, sir, you're wrong, they ain't no 'dogs.' I'm
not through tellin' yet;
You'll take that name right back again, or else jest
out you get!
You'll take that name right back when you hear
all this yarn, I bet.

"It happened that same autumn, when some
Whites was comin' in,
I heard the old Red River carts a-kickin'
up a din,
So I went over to their camp to see an English
skin.

"They said, 'They'd had an awful scare from
                    Injuns,' an' they swore
That savages had come around the very night
                    before
A-brandishing their tomahawks an' painted up for
                    war.

"But when their plucky Englishmen had put a bit
                    of lead
Right through the heart of one of them, an' rolled
                    him over, dead,
The other cowards said that they had come on peace
                    instead.

" 'That they (the Whites) had lost some stores,
                    from off their little pack,
An' that the Red they peppered dead had followed
                    up their track,
Because he'd found the packages an' came TO GIVE
                    THEM BACK.'

" 'Oh!' they said, 'they were quite sorry, but it
                    wasn't like as if
They had killed a decent Whiteman by mistake or
                    in a tiff,
It was only some old Injun dog that lay there stark
                    an' stiff.

"I said, 'You are the meanest dogs that ever yet
I seen,'
Then I rolled the body over as it lay out on the
green;
I peered into the face — My God! 'twas poor old
Wolverine."

❦ THE BALLAD OF YAADA
(A Legend of the Pacific Coast)

There are fires on Lulu Island, and the sky is
                    opalescent
        With the pearl and purple tinting from the
                    smouldering of peat.
And the Dream Hills lift their summits in a sweeping,
                    hazy crescent,
        With the Capilano canyon at their feet.

There are fires on Lulu Island, and the smoke,
                    uplifting, lingers
        In a faded scarf of fragrance as it creeps across
                    the day,
And the Inlet and the Narrows blur beneath its
                    silent fingers,
        And the canyon is enfolded in its grey.

But the sun its face is veiling like a cloistered nun
                    at vespers;
        As towards the altar candles of the night a censer
                    swings,
And the echo of tradition wakes from slumbering
                    and whispers,
        Where the Capilano river sobs and sings.

It was Yaada, lovely Yaada, who first taught the
stream its sighing,
For 'twas silent till her coming, and 'twas
voiceless as the shore;
But throughout the great forever it will sing the
song undying
That the lips of lovers sing for evermore.

He was chief of all the Squamish, and he ruled the
coastal waters —
And he warred upon her people in the distant
Charlotte Isles;
She, a winsome basket weaver, daintiest of Haida
daughters,
Made him captive to her singing and her smiles.

Till his hands forgot to havoc and his weapons lost
their lusting,
Till his stormy eyes allured her from the land of
Totem Poles,
Till she followed where he called her, followed with
a woman's trusting,
To the canyon where the Capilano rolls.

And the women of the Haidas plied in vain their
                     magic power,
    Wailed for many moons her absence, wailed for
                        many moons their prayer,
"Bring her back, O Squamish foeman, bring to us
                     our Yaada flower!"
    But the silence only answered their despair.

But the men were swift to battle, swift to cross
                     the coastal water,
    Swift to war and swift of weapon, swift to paddle
                       trackless miles,
Crept with stealth along the canyon, stole her from
                     her love and brought her
    Once again unto the distant Charlotte Isles.

But she faded, ever faded, and her eyes were
                     ever turning
    Southward toward the Capilano, while her voice
                       had hushed its song,
And her riven heart repeated words that on her
                     lips were burning:
    "Not to friend — but unto foeman I belong.

❦ 91

*"Give me back my Squamish lover — though you
            hate, I still must love him.
    "Give me back the rugged canyon where my heart
            must ever be —
Where his lodge awaits my coming, and the Dream
            Hills lift above him,
    And the Capilano learned its song from me."*

*But through long-forgotten seasons, moons too many
            to be numbered,
    He yet waited by the canyon — she called
            across the years,
And the soul within the river, though centuries had
            slumbered,
    Woke to sob a song of woman's tears.*

*For her little, lonely spirit sought the Capilano
            canyon,
    When she died among the Haidas in the land
            of Totem Poles,
And you yet may hear her singing to her lover-like
            companion,
    If you listen to the river as it rolls.*

But 'tis only when the pearl and purple smoke is
idly swinging
From the fires on Lulu Island to the hazy
mountain crest,
That the undertone of sobbing echoes through the
river's singing,
In the Capilano canyon of the West.

Crown of her, young Vancouver; crest of her,
old Quebec;
Atlantic and far Pacific sweeping her, keel
to deck.
North of her, ice and arctics; southward, a
rival's stealth;
Aloft, her Empire's pennant; below, her nation's
wealth.
Daughter of men and markets, bearing within her
hold,
Appraised at highest value, cargoes of grain and
gold.

Out of the night and the north,
                    Savage of breed and of bone,
Shaggy and swift comes the yelping band,
Freighters of fur from the voiceless land
                    That sleeps in the Arctic zone.

Laden with skins from the north,
                    Beaver and bear and raccoon,
Marten and mink from the polar belts,
Otter and ermine and sable pelts —
                    The spoils of the hunter's moon.

Out of the night and the north,
                    Sinewy, fearless and fleet,
Urging the pack through the pathless snow,
The Indian driver, calling low,
                    Follows with moccasined feet.

Ships of the night and the north,
                    Freighters on prairies and plains,
Carrying cargoes from field and flood
They scent the trail through their wild red blood,
                    The wolfish blood in their veins.

West wind, blow from your prairie nest,
Blow from the mountains, blow from the west.
The sail is idle, the sailor too;
O! wind of the west, we wait for you.
            Blow, blow!
I have wooed you so,
But never a favour you bestow.
You rock your cradle the hills between,
But scorn to notice my white lateen.

I stow the sail, unship the mast:
I wooed you long but my wooing's past;
My paddle will lull you into rest.
O! drowsy wind of the drowsy west,
            Sleep, sleep,
By your mountain steep,
Or down where the prairie grasses sweep!
Now fold in slumber your laggard wings,
For soft is the song my paddle sings.

August is laughing across the sky,
Laughing while paddle, canoe and I,
            Drift, drift,
Where the hills uplift
On either side of the current swift.

The river rolls in its rocky bed;
My paddle is plying its way ahead!
       Dip, dip,
While the waters flip
In foam as over their breast we slip.

And oh, the river runs swifter now;
The eddies circle about my bow.
       Swirl, Swirl!
How the ripples curl
In many a dangerous pool awhirl!

And forward far the rapids roar,
Fretting their margin for evermore.
       Dash, dash,
With a mighty crash,
They seethe, and boil, and bound, and splash.

Be strong, O paddle! be brave, canoe!
The reckless waves you must plunge into.
       Reel, reel.
On your trembling keel,
But never a fear my craft will feel.

We've raced the rapid, we're far ahead!
The river slips through its silent bed.
          Sway, sway,
As the bubbles spray
And fall in tinkling tunes away.

And up on the hills against the sky,
A fir tree rocking its lullaby,
          Swings, swings,
Its emerald wings,
Swelling the song that my paddle sings.

Now for a careful beach atween the towering
    Gray rocks that yawn like tombs.
Aft lies the lake, blurred by our paddles' scouring,
    Forward, the portage looms.
        Beyond its fastnessess, a river creeping,
        Then — rapids leaping.

Now for a bracing up of stalwart shoulders,
    And now, a load to lift.
An uphill tramp through tangled briars and boulders,
    The irksome weight to shift.
        And through it all, the far incessant calling
        Of waters falling.

What of the heat? The toil? The sun's red glaring?
    The blistered fingers too?
What of the muscles teased and strained in bearing
    The fearless, fleet canoe?
        Brief is the labour, then the wild sweet laughter
        Of rapids after.

Night 'neath the northern skies, lone, black, and grim:
Naught but the starlight lies 'twixt heaven, and him.

Of man no need has he, of God, no prayer;
He and his Deity are brothers there.

Above his bivouac the firs fling down
Through branches gaunt and black, their needles brown.

Afar some mountain streams, rockbound and fleet,
Sing themselves through his dreams in cadence sweet,

The pine trees whispering, the heron's cry,
The plover's passing wing, his lullaby.

And blinking overhead the white stars keep
    Watch o'er his hemlock bed — his sinless sleep.

At husking time the tassel fades
To brown above the yellow blades,
Whose rustling sheath enswathes the corn
That bursts its chrysalis in scorn
Longer to lie in prison shades.

Among the merry lads and maids
The creaking ox-cart slowly wades
Twixt stalks and stubble, sacked and torn
At husking time.

The prying pilot crow persuades
The flock to join in thieving raids;
The sly racoon with craft inborn
His portion steals; from plenty's horn
His pouch the saucy chipmunk lades
At husking time.

In Muskoka

Lichens of green and grey on every side;
And green and grey the rocks beneath our feet;
Above our heads the canvas stretching wide;
And over all, enchantment rare and sweet.

Fair Rosseau slumbers in an atmosphere
That kisses her to passionless soft dreams.
O! joy of living we have found thee here,
And life lacks nothing, so complete it seems.

The velvet air, stirred by some elfin wings,
Comes swinging up the waters and then stills
Its voice so low that floating by it sings
Like distant harps among the distant hills.

Across the lake the rugged islands lie,
Fir-crowned and grim; and further in the view
Some shadows seeming swung 'twixt cloud and sky,
Are countless shores, a symphony of blue.

Some northern sorceress, when day is done,
Hovers where cliffs uplift their gaunt grey steeps,
Bewitching to vermilion Rosseau's sun,
That in a liquid mass of rubies sleeps.

Muskoka

A stream of tender gladness,
Of filmy sun, and opal tinted skies;
Of warm midsummer air that lightly lies
                    In mystic rings,
                        Where softly swings
The music of a thousand wings
That almost tones to sadness.

Midway 'twixt earth and heaven,
A bubble in the pearly air, I seem
To float upon the sapphire floor, a dream
                    Of clouds of snow,
                        Above, below,
Drift with my drifting, dim and slow,
As twilight drifts to even.

The little fern-leaf, bending
Upon the brink, its green reflection greets,
And kisses soft the shadow that it meets
                    With touch so fine,
                        The border line
The keenest vision can't define;
So perfect is the blending.

The far, fir trees that cover
The brownish hills with needles green and gold,
The arching elms o'erhead, vinegrown and old,
   Repictured are
   Beneath me far,
Where not a ripple moves to mar
Shades underneath, or over.

Mine is the undertone;
The beauty, strength, and power of the land
Will never stir or bend at my command;
   But all the shade
   Is marred or made,
If I but dip my paddle blade;
And it is mine alone.

O! pathless world of seeming!
O! pathless life of mine whose deep ideal
Is more my own than ever was the real.
   For others Fame
   And Love's red flame,
And yellow gold: I only claim
The shadows and the dreaming.

A dash of yellow sand,
Wind-scattered and sun-tanned;
Some waves that curl and cream along the margin of the
strand;
And, creeping close to these
Long shores that lounge at ease,
Old Erie rocks and ripples to a fresh sou'-western breeze.

A sky of blue and grey;
Some stormy clouds that play
At scurrying up with ragged edge, then laughing blow away,
Just leaving in their trail
Some snatches of a gale;
To whistling summer winds we lift a single daring sail.

O! wind so sweet and swift,
O! danger-freighted gift
Bestowed on Erie with her waves that foam and fall and lift,
We laugh in your wild face,
And break into a race
With flying clouds and tossing gulls that weave and interlace.

What dream you in the night-time
          When you whisper to the moon?
What say you in the morning?
          What do you sing at noon?
When I hear your voice uplifting,
Like a breeze through branches sifting,
And your ripples softly drifting
          To the August airs a-tune.

Lend me your happy laughter,
          Ste. Marie, as you leap;
Your peace that follows after
          Where through the isles you creep.
Give to me your splendid dashing,
Give your sparkles and your splashing,
Your uphurling waves down crashing,
          Then, your aftermath of sleep.

Halifax sits on her hills by the sea
            In the might of her pride,—
Invincible, terrible, beautiful, she
            With a sword at her side.

To right and to left of her, battlements rear
            And fortresses frown;
While she sits on her throne without favour or fear
            With her cannon as crown.

Coast guard and sentinel, watch of the weal
            Of a nation she keeps;
But her hand is encased in a gauntlet of steel,
            And her thunder but sleeps.

The long red flats stretch open to the sky,
Breathing their moisture on the August air.
The seaweeds cling with flesh-like fingers where
The rocks give shelter that the sands deny;
And wrapped in all her summer harmonies
St. Andrews sleeps beside her sleeping seas.

The far-off shores swim blue and indistinct,
Like half-lost memories of some old dream.
The listless waves that catch each sunny gleam
Are idling up the waterways land-linked,
And, yellowing along the harbour's breast,
The light is leaping shoreward from the west.

And naked-footed children, tripping down,
Light with young laughter, daily come at eve
To gather dulse and sea clams and then heave
Their loads, returning laden to the town,
Leaving a strange grey silence when they go,—
The silence of the sands when tides are low.

Up the dusk-enfolded prairie,
             Foot-falls, soft and sly,
Velvet cushioned, wild and wary,
             Then — the coyote's cry.

Rush of hoofs, and roar and rattle,
             Beasts of blood and breed,
Twenty thousand frightened cattle,
             Then — the wild stampede.

Pliant lasso circling wider
             In the frenzied flight —
Loping horse and cursing rider,
             Plunging through the night.

Rim of dawn the darkness losing
             Trail of blackened soil;
Perfume of the sage brush oozing
             On the air like oil.

Foothills to the Rockies lifting
             Brown, and blue, and green,
Warm Alberta sunlight drifting
             Over leagues between.

That's the country of the ranges,
             Plain and prairie land,
And the God who never changes
             Holds it in His hand.

Born on the breast of the prairie, she smiles to her
sire — the sun,
Robed in the wealth of her wheat-lands, gift of her
mothering soil,
Affluence knocks at her gateways, opulence waits
to be won.
Nuggets of gold are her acres, yielding and yellow
with spoil,
Dream of the hungry millions, dawn of the food-
filled age,
Over the starving tale of want her fingers have
turned the page;
Nations will nurse at her storehouse, and God gives
her grain for wage.

Not of the seething cities with their swarming
          human hives,
Their fetid airs, their reeking streets, their dwarfed
          and poisoned lives,
Not of the buried yesterdays, but of the days to be,
The glory and the gateway of the yellow West is she.

The Northern Lights dance down her plains with soft
          and silvery feet,
The sunrise gilds her prairies when the dawn and
          daylight meet;
And beyond her western windows the sublime old
          mountains sleep.

The Redman haunts her portals, and the Paleface
          treads her streets,
The Indian's stealthy footstep with the course of
          commerce meets,
And hunters whisper vaguely of the half forgotten
          tales
Of phantom herds of bison lurking on her midnight
          trails.

Not hers the lore of olden lands, their laurels and
their bays;
But what are these, compared to one of all her
perfect days?
For naught can buy the jewel that upon her fore-
head lies —
The cloudless sapphire Heaven of her territorial
skies.

A trail upwinds from Golden;
It leads to a land God only knows,
To the land of eternal frozen snows,
That trail unknown and olden.

And they tell a tale that is strange and wild —
Of a lovely and lonely mountain child
That went up the trail from Golden.

A child in the sweet of her womanhood,
Beautiful, tender, grave and good
As the saints in time long olden.

And the days count not, nor the weeks avail;
For the child that went up the mountain trail
Came never again to Golden.

And the watchers wept in the midnight gloom,
Where the canyons yawn and the Selkirks loom,
For the love that they knew of olden.

And April dawned, with its suns aflame,
And the eagles wheeled and the vultures came
And poised o'er the town of Golden.

God of the white eternal peaks,
Guard the dead while the vulture seeks! —
God of the days so olden.

For only God in His greatness knows
Where the mountain holly above her grows,
On the trail that leads from Golden.

(Thunder Bay, Lake Superior)

When did you sink to your dreamless sleep
  Out there in your thunder bed?
Where the tempests sweep,
And the waters leap,
  And the storms rage overhead.

Were you lying there on your couch alone
  Ere Egypt and Rome were born?
Ere the Age of Stone,
Or the world had known
  The Man with the Crown of Thorn.

The winds screech down from the open west,
  And the thunders beat and break
On the amethyst
Of your rugged breast, —
  But you never arise or wake.

You have locked your past, and you keep the key
  In your heart 'neath the westing sun,
Where the mighty sea
And its shores will be
  Storm-swept till the world is done.

At Crow's Nest Pass the mountains rend
Themselves apart, the rivers wend
    A lawless course about their feet,
    And breaking into torrents beat
In useless fury where they blend
       At Crow's Nest Pass.

The nesting eagles, wise, discreet,
Wings up the gorge's lone retreat
And makes some barren crag her friend
       At Crow's Nest Pass.

Uncertain clouds, half-high, suspend
Their shifting vapours, and contend
    With rocks that suffer not defeat;
    And snows, and suns, and mad winds meet
To battle where the cliffs defend
       At Crow's Nest Pass.

Sob of fall, and song of forest, come you here on
haunting quest,
Calling through the seas and silence, from God's
country of the west.
Where the mountain pass is narrow, and the torrent
white and strong,
Down its rocky-throated canyon, sings its golden-
throated song.

You are singing there together through the God-
begotten nights,
And the leaning stars are listening above the
distant heights
That lift like points of opal in the crescent
coronet
About whose golden setting sweeps the trail
to Lillooet.

Trail that winds and trail that wanders, like a
cobweb hanging high,
Just a hazy thread outlining mid-way of the stream
and sky,
Where the Fraser River canyon yawns its pathway
to the sea,
But half the world has shouldered up between its
song and me.

Here, the placid English August, and the sea-
        encircled miles,
There — God's copper-coloured sunshine beating
        through the lonely aisles
Where the waterfalls and forest voice for ever
        their duet,
And call across the canyon on the trail
        to Lillooet.

❦ A TOAST

There's wine in the cup, Vancouver,
  And there's warmth in my heart for you,
While I drink to your health, your youth, and your
        wealth,
  And the things that you yet will do.
In a vintage rare and olden,
  With a flavour fine and keen,
Fill the glass to the edge, while I stand up to pledge
  My faith to my western queen.

Then here's a Ho! Vancouver, in wine of the
        bonniest hue,
  With a hand on my hip and the cup at my lip,
And a love in my life for you.
  For you are a jolly good fellow, with a great,
        big heart, I know;
So I drink this toast
To the "Queen of the Coast."
  Vancouver, here's a Ho!

And here's to the days that are coming,
  And here's to the days that are gone,
And here's to your gold and your spirit bold,
  And your luck that has held its own;
And here's to your hands so sturdy,
  And here's to your hearts so true,
And here's to the speed of the day decreed
  That brings me again to you.

❦ 119

Then here's a Ho! Vancouver, in wine of the
                    bonniest hue,
     With a hand on my hip and the cup at my lip,
And a love in my life for you.
          For you are a jolly good fellow, with a great,
                    big heart, I know;
So I drink this toast
To the "Queen of the Coast."
          Vancouver, here's a Ho!

A thin wet sky, that yellows at the rim,
And meets with sun-lost lip the marsh's brim.

The pools low lying, dank with moss and mould,
Glint through their mildews like large cups of gold.

Among the wild rice in the still lagoon,
In monotone the lizard shrills his tune.

The wild goose, homing, seeks a sheltering,
Where rushes grow, and oozing lichens cling.

Late cranes with heavy wing, and lazy flight,
Sail up the silence with the nearing night.

And like a spirit, swathed in some soft veil,
Steals twilight and its shadows o'er the swale.

Hushed lie the sedges, and the vapours creep,
Thick, grey and humid, while the marshes sleep.

Little Lady Icicle is dreaming in the north-land
And gleaming in the north-land, her pillow all aglow;
  For the frost has come and found her
  With an ermine robe around her
Where little Lady Icicle lies dreaming in the snow.

Little Lady Icicle is waking in the north-land,
And shaking in the north-land her pillow to and fro;
  And the hurricane a-skirling
  Sends the feathers all a-whirling
Where little Lady Icicle is waking in the snow.

Little Lady Icicle is laughing in the north-land,
And quaffing in the north-land her wines that overflow;
  All the lakes and rivers crusting
  That her finger-tips are dusting,
Where little Lady Icicle is laughing in the snow.

Little Lady Icicle is singing in the north-land,
And bringing from the north-land a music wild and low;
  And the fairies watch and listen
  Where her silver slippers glisten,
As little Lady Icicle goes singing through the snow.

An Etching

A meadow brown; across the yonder edge
A zigzag fence is ambling; here a wedge
Of underbush has cleft its course in twain,
Till where beyond it staggers up again;
The long, grey rails stretch in a broken line
Their ragged length of rough, split forest pine,
And in their zigzag tottering have reeled
In drunken efforts to enclose the field,
Which carries on its breast, September born,
A patch of rustling, yellow, Indian corn.
Beyond its shrivelled tassels, perched upon
The topmost rail, sits Joe, the settler's son,
A little semi-savage boy of nine.
Now dozing in the warmth of Nature's wine,
His face the sun has tampered with, and wrought,
By heated kisses, mischief, and has brought
Some vagrant freckles, while from here and there
A few wild locks of vagabond brown hair
Escape the old straw hat the sun looks through,
And blinks to meet his Irish eyes of blue.
Barefooted, innocent of coat or vest,
His grey checked shirt unbuttoned at his chest,
Both hardy hands within their usual nest —
His breeches pockets — so, he waits to rest
His little fingers, somewhat tired and worn,

That all day long were husking Indian corn.
His drowsy lids snap at some trivial sound,
With lazy yawns he slips towards the ground,
Then with an idle whistle lifts his load
And shambles home along the country road
That stretches on, fringed out with stumps and weeds,
And finally unto the backwoods leads,
Where forests wait with giant trunk and bough
The axe of pioneer, the settler's plough.

From out the west, where darkling storm-clouds float,
The 'waking wind pipes soft its rising note.

From out the west, o'erhung with fringes grey,
The wind preludes with sighs its roundelay,

Then blowing, singing, piping, laughing loud,
It scurries on before the grey storm-cloud;

Across the hollow and along the hill
It whips and whirls among the maples, till

With boughs upbent, and green of leaves blown wide,
The silver shines upon their underside.

A gusty freshening of humid air,
With showers laden, and with fragrance rare;

And now a little sprinkle, with a dash
Of great cool drops that fall with sudden splash;

Then over field and hollow, grass and grain,
The loud, crisp whiteness of the nearing rain.

Pillowed and hushed on the silent plain,
Wrapped in her mantle of golden grain,

Wearied of pleasuring weeks away,
Summer is lying asleep to-day, —

Where winds come sweet from the wild-rose briers
And the smoke of the far-off prairie fires;

Yellow her hair as the goldenrod,
And brown her cheeks as the prairie sod;

Purple her eyes as the mists that dream
At the edge of some laggard sun-drowned stream;

But over their depths the lashes sweep,
For Summer is lying to-day asleep.

The north wind kisses her rosy mouth,
His rival frowns in the far-off south,

And comes caressing her sunburnt cheek,
And Summer awakes for one short week, —

Awakes and gathers her wealth of grain,
Then sleeps and dreams for a year again.

All the long day the vapours played
    At blindfold in the city streets,
Their elfin fingers caught and stayed
    The sunbeams, as they wound their sheets
Into a filmy barricade
    'Twixt earth and where the sunlight beats.

A vagrant band of mischiefs these,
    With wings of grey and cobweb gown;
They live along the edge of seas,
    And creeping out on foot of down,
They chase and frolic, frisk and tease
    At blind-man's buff with all the town.

And when at eventide the sun
    Breaks with a glory through their grey,
The vapour-fairies, one by one,
    Outspread their wings and float away
In clouds of colouring, that run
    Wine-like along the rim of day.

Athwart the beauty and the breast
    Of purpling airs they twirl and twist,
Then float away to some far rest,
    Leaving the skies all colour-kiss't —
A glorious and a golden West
    That greets the Lifting of the Mist.

Like a grey shadow lurking in the light,
He ventures forth along the edge of night;
With silent foot he scouts the coulie's rim
And scents the carrion awaiting him.
His savage eyeballs lurid with a flare
Seen but in unfed beasts which leave their lair
To wrangle with their fellows for a meal
Of bones ill-covered. Sets he forth to steal,
To search and snarl and forage hungrily;
A worthless prairie vagabond is he.
Luckless the settler's heifer which astray
Falls to his fangs and violence a prey;
Useless her blatant calling when his teeth
Are fast upon her quivering flank — beneath
His fell voracity she falls and dies
With inarticulate and piteous cries,
Unheard, unheeded in the barren waste,
To be devoured with savage greed and haste.
Up the horizon once again he prowls
And far across its desolation howls;
Sneaking and satisfied his lair he gains
And leaves her bones to bleach upon the plains.

Mine is the fate to watch the evening star
                    In yonder dome,
Descending slowly through the cobweb bar
That girts the twilight mysteries afar,
                    Above your home.

Mine is the fate to turn toward the west
                    When falls the dew.
When dips the sun beyond the woodland crest
At vesper hour, I think, loved and best,
                    Alone of you.

And mine the happy fate to live for aye
                    Within the dream
Of knowing that the sun lights not the day
But that some little thoughts of yours to me will stray,
                    My little Jean.

They both live side by side, among
The wooded banks of endless song
Where wild birds carol all day long.

The iris grows beneath the ledge
Of bank, all overgrown with sedge
That creeps along the river's edge.

My little girl, so like that flower,
Strong in her purity of power,
Fidelity her richest dower.

Her sister trim, the iris blue,
With blossoms clothed in Heaven's hue,
So like her life, so tried and true.

They both live where they daily meet
Temptations, through their lives so sweet,
An undercurrent 'round their feet.

The streams of love and truth to blend,
A sweetness Heaven alone can send
The iris, and my little friend.

Serene dark pool, with all your colours dulled,
Your dreamless waves by twilight slumber lulled;
Your warmth that flamed because the hot sun hushed
Your lip vermilion that his kisses crushed;
Wan are the tints he left of gold and gem,
For dusk's soft cloudy greys have smothered them.
Where yonder shore's tree-terraced outlines melt,
The shadows circle like a velvet belt;
And down, far down within the sable deep,
A white star-soul awakens from his sleep.
O, little lake with twilight interlinked,
Your darkling shores, your margin indistinct —
More in your depth's uncertainty their lies
Than when you image all the sunset dyes.
Like to the poet's soul you seem to be,
A depth no hand can touch, no eye can see.
And melancholy's dusky clouds drift through
The singer's songs, as twilight drifts o'er you.
O, life that saddens for the colours fled,
Within your depths a diamond 'wakes instead.
Perchance in spheres remote, and fair and far,
There breathes a twin soul to my soul's white star
Or have we touched already, and passed by
Unconscious that affinity was nigh?
O, soul, perchance so near me, yet unknown,
Some day we'll wake within fate's velvet zone.

Idles the night wind through the dreaming firs,
                    That waking murmur low,
As some lost melody returning stirs
                    The love of long ago;
And through the far cool distance, zephyr fanned.
The moon is sinking into shadow-land.

The troubled night-bird, calling plaintively,
                    Wanders on restless wing;
The cedars, chanting vespers to the sea,
                    Await its answering,
That comes in wash of waves along the strand.
The while the moon slips into shadow-land.

O! soft responsive voices of the night
                    I join your minstrelsy,
And call across the fading silver light
                    As something calls to me;
I may not all your meaning understand,
But I have touched your soul in shadow-land.

To-night the west o'er-brims with warmest dyes;
             Its chalice overflows
With pools of purple colouring the skies,
             Aflood with gold and rose;
And some hot soul seems throbbing close to mine,
As sinks the sun within that world of wine.

I seem to hear a bar of music float
             And swoon into the west;
My ear can scarcely catch the whispered note,
             But something in my breast
Blends with that srtain, till both accord in one,
As cloud and colour blend at set of sun.

And twilight comes with grey and restful eyes,
             As ashes follow flame.
But O! I heard a voice from those rich skies
             Call tenderly my name;
It was as if some priestly fingers stole
In benedictions o'er my lonely soul.

I know not why, but all my being longed
             And leapt at that sweet call;
My heart outreached its arms, all passion thronged
             And beat against Fate's wall,
Crying in utter homesickness to be
Near to a heart that loves and leans to me.

So near at hand (our eyes o'erlooked its nearness
In search of distant things)
A dear dream lay — perchance to grow in dearness
Had we but felt its wings
Astir. The air our very breathing fanned
It was so near at hand.

Once, many days ago, we almost held it,
The love we so desired;
But our shut eyes saw not, and fate dispelled it
Before our pulses fired
To flame, and errant fortune bade us stand
Hand almost touching hand.

I sometimes think had we two been discerning,
The by-path hid away
From others' eyes had then revealed it turning
Thus, nor led astray
Our footsteps, guiding us into love's land
That lay so near at hand.

So near at hand, dear heart, could we have known it!
Throughout those dreamy hours,
Had either loved, or loving had we shown it.
Response had sure been ours;
We did not know that heart could heart command,
And love so near at hand!

What then availed the red wine's subtle glisten?
We passed it blindly by,
And now what profit that we wait and listen
Each for the other's heart beat? Ah! the cry
Of love o'erlooked still lingers, you and I
Sought heaven afar, we did not understand
T was — once so near at hand.

It is dusk on the Lost Lagoon,
And we two dreaming the dusk away,
Beneath the drift of a twilight grey,
Beneath the drowse of an ending day,
    And the curve of a golden moon.

It is dark in the Lost Lagoon,
And gone are the depths of haunting blue,
The grouping gulls, and the old canoe,
The singing firs, and the dusk and — you,
    And gone is the golden moon.

O! lure of the Lost Lagoon, —
I dream to-night that my paddle blurs
The purple shade where the seaweed stirs,
I hear the call of the singing firs
    In the hush of the golden moon.

I am sailing to the leeward,
Where the current runs to seaward
                Soft and slow,
Where the sleeping river grasses
Brush my paddle as it passes
                To and fro.

On the shore the heat is shaking
All the golden sands awaking
                In the cove;
And the quaint sand-piper, winging
O'er the shallows, ceases singing
                When I move.

On the water's idle pillow
Sleeps the overhanging willow,
                Green and cool;
Where the rushes lift their burnished
Oval heads from out the tarnished
                Emerald pool.

Where the very silence slumbers,
Water lilies grow in numbers,
                Pure and pale;
All the morning they have rested,
Amber crowned, and pearly crested,
                Fair and frail.

Here, impossible romances,
Indefinable sweet fancies,
                    Cluster round;
But they do not mar the sweetness
Of this still September fleetness
                    With a sound.

I can scarce discern the meeting
Of the shore and stream retreating,
                    So remote;
For the laggard river, dozing,
Only wakes from its reposing
                    Where I float.
Where the river mists are rising,
All the foliage baptizing
                    With their spray;
There the sun gleams far and faintly,
With a shadow soft and saintly,
                    In its ray.

And the perfume of some burning
Far-off brushwood, ever turning
                    To exhale
All its smoky fragrance dying,
In the arms of evening lying,
                    Where I sail.

My canoe is growing lazy,
In the atmosphere so hazy,
               While I dream;
Half in slumber I am guiding,
Eastward indistinctly gliding
               Down the stream.

To-night I hunger so,
Beloved one, to know
If you recall and crave again the dream
That haunted our canoe,
And wove its witchcraft through
Our hearts as 'neath the northern night we sailed
the northern stream.

Ah! dear, if only we
As yesternight could be
Afloat within that light and lonely shell,
To drift in silence till
Heart-hushed, and lulled and still
The moonlight through the melting air flung forth
its fatal spell.

The dusky summer night,
The path of gold and white
The moon had cast across the river's breast,
The shores in shadows clad,
The far-away, half-sad
Sweet singing of the whip-poor-will, all soothed our
souls to rest.

You trusted I could feel
My arm as strong as steel,
So still your upturned face, so calm your breath,
While circling eddies curled,
While laughing rapids whirled
From boulder unto boulder, till they dashed
                    themselves to death.

Your splendid eyes aflame
Put heaven's stars to shame,
Your god-like head so near my lap was laid —
My hand is burning where
It touched your wind-blown hair,
As sweeping to the rapids verge, I changed my
                    paddle blade.

The boat obeyed my hand,
Till wearied with its grand
Wild anger, all the river lay aswoon,
And as my paddle dipped,
Thro' pools of pearl it slipped
And swept beneath a shore of shade, beneath a
                    velvet moon.

To-night again dream you
Our spirit-winged canoe
Is listening to the rapids purling past?
Where, in delirium reeled
Our maddened hearts that kneeled
To idolize the perfect world, to taste of love
at last.

All yesterday the thought of you was resting in
        my soul,
And when sleep wandered o'er the world that very
        thought she stole
To fill my dreams with splendour such as stars could
        not eclipse,
And in the morn I wakened with your name upon
        my lips.

Awakened, my beloved, to the morning of
        your eyes,
Your splendid eyes, so full of clouds, wherein a
        shadow tries
To overcome the flame that melts into the world
        of grey,
As coming suns dissolve the dark that veils the edge
        of day.

Cool drifts the air at dawn of day, cool lies the
        sleeping dew,
But all my heart is burning, for it woke from dreams
        of you;
And O! these longing eyes of mine look out and
        only see
A dying night, a waking day, and calm on all
        but me.

So gently creeps the morning through the
                    heavy air,
The dawn grey-garbed and velvet-shod is wandering
                    everywhere
To wake the slumber-laden hours that leave their
                    dreamless rest,
With outspread, laggard wings to court the pillows
                    of the west.

Up from the earth a moisture steals with odours
                    fresh and soft,
A smell of moss and grasses warm with dew, and
                    far aloft
The stars are growing colourless, while drooping in
                    the west,
A late, wan moon is paling in a sky of
                    amethyst.

The passing of the shadows, as they waft their
                    pinions near,
Has stirred a tender wind within the night-hushed
                    atmosphere,
That in its homeless wanderings sobs in an
                    undertone
An echo to my heart that sobbing calls
                    for you alone.

The night is gone, belovéd, and another day set
free,
Another day of hunger for the one I may
not see.
What care I for the perfect dawn? the blue and
empty skies?
The night is always mine without the morning of
your eyes.

The night-long shadows faded into gray,
    Then silvered into glad and gold sunlight
Because you came to me, like a new day
    Born of the beauty of an autumn night.

The silence that enfolded me so long
    Stirred to the sweetest music life has known,
Because you came, and coming woke the song
    That slumbered through the years I was alone.

So have you brought me silver from the shade,
    The music and the laughter and the day.
So have you come to me, and coming made
    This life of mine a blossom-bordered way.

What of the days when we two dreamed together?
                    Days marvellously fair,
As lightsome as a skyward floating feather
                    Sailing on summer air —
Summer, summer, that came drifting through
Fate's hand to me, to you.

What of the days, my dear? I sometimes wonder
                    If you too wish this sky
Could be the blue we sailed so softly under,
                    In that sun-kissed July;
Sailed in the warm and yellow afternoon,
With hearts in touch and tune.

Have you no longing to re-live the dreaming,
                    Adrift in my canoe?
To watch my paddle blade all wet and gleaming
                    Cleaving the waters through?
To lie wind-blown and wave-caressed, until
Your restless pulse grows still?

Do you not long to listen to the purling
                    Of foam athwart the keel?
To hear the nearing rapids softly swirling
                    Among their stones, to feel
The boat's unsteady tremor as it braves
The wild and snarling waves?

What need of question, what of your replying?
               Oh! well I know that you
Would toss the world away to be but lying
               Again in my canoe,
In listless indolence entranced and lost,
Wave-rocked, and passion tossed.

Ah me! my paddle failed me in the steering
               Across love's shoreless seas;
All reckless, I had ne'er a thought of fearing
               Such dreary days as these,
When through the self-same rapids we dash by,
My lone canoe and I.

Pine trees sobbing a weird unrest
     In saddened strains,
Crows flying slowly into the West
     As daylight wanes,
Breezes that die in a stifled breath:
O happy breezes, embraced by death.

Fir trees reaching toward the sky
     In giant form
Lift me up into your arms, that I
     May brave the storm.
O darling, unclasp your fair, warm hand;
'Tis better I should misunderstand.

Turn in pity those tender eyes
     Away from me.
The burning sorrow that in them lies
     Is misery.
O, gentlest pleader my life has known,
Goodbye. The night and I are alone.

Soulless is all humanity to me
To-night. My keenest longing is to be
Alone, alone with God's grey earth that seems
Pulse of my pulse and consort of my dreams.

To-night my soul desires no fellowship,
Or fellow-being; crave I but to slip
Thro' space on space, till flesh no more can bind,
And I may quit for aye my fellow kind.

Let me but feel athwart my cheek the lash
Of whipping wind, but hear the torrent dash
Adown the mountain steep, 'twere more my choice
Than touch of human hand, than human voice.

Let me but wander on the shore night-stilled,
Drinking its darkness till my soul is filled;
The breathing of the salt sea on my hair,
My outstretched hands but grasping empty air.

Let me but feel the pulse of Nature's soul
Athrob on mine, let seas and thunders roll
O'er night and me; sands whirl; winds, waters beat;
For God's grey earth has no cheap counterfeit.

My heart forgot its God for love of you,
*   And you forgot me, other loves to learn;*
Now through a wilderness of thorn and rue
*   Back to my God I turn.*

And just because my God forgets the past,
*   And in forgetting does not ask to know*
Why I once left His arms for yours, at last
*   Back to my God I go.*

Because, dear Christ, your tender, wounded arm
    Bends back the brier that edges life's long way.
That no hurt comes to heart, to soul no harm,
    I do not feel the thorns so much to-day.

Because I never knew your care to tire,
    Your hand to weary guiding me aright,
Because you walk before and crush the brier,
    It does not pierce my feet so much to-night.

Because so often you have hearkened to
    My selfish prayers, I ask but one thing now,
That these harsh hands of mine add not unto
    The crown of thorns upon your bleeding brow.

I may not go to-night to Bethlehem,
Nor follow star-directed ways, nor tread
The paths wherein the shepherds walked, that led
To Christ, and peace, and God's good will to men.

I may not hear the Herald Angel's song
Peal through the Oriental skies, nor see
The wonder of that Heavenly company
Announce the King the world had waited long.

The manger throne I may not kneel before,
Or see how man to God is reconciled,
Through pure St. Mary's purer, holier child;
The human Christ these eyes may not adore.

I may not carry frankincense and myrrh
With adoration to the Holy One;
Nor gold have I to give the Perfect Son,
To be with those wise kings a worshipper.

Not mine the joy that Heaven sent to them,
For ages since Time swung and locked his gates,
But I may kneel without — the star still waits
To guide me on to holy Bethlehem.

Unknown to you, I walk the cheerless shore.
　　The cutting blast, the hurl of biting brine
May freeze, and still, and bind the waves at war,
　　Ere you will ever know, O! Heart of mine,
That I have sought, reflected in the blue
　　Of these sea depths, some shadow of your eyes;
Have hoped the laughing waves would sing of you,
　　But this is all my starving sight descries —

I

Far out at sea a sail
　　Bends to the freshening breeze,
Yields to the rising gale
　　That sweeps the seas;

II

Yields, as a bird wind-tossed,
　　To saltish waves that fling
Their spray, whose rime and frost
　　Like crystals cling

III

To canvas, mast and spar,
　　Till, gleaming like a gem,
She sinks beyond the far
　　Horizon's hem.

IV
Lost to my longing sight,
    And nothing left to me
Save an oncoming night, —
    An empty sea.

Sleep, with her tender balm, her touch so kind,
                    Has passed me by;
Afar I see her vesture, velvet-lined,
                    Float silently;
O! Sleep, my tired eyes had need of thee!
Is thy sweet kiss not meant to-night for me?

Peace, with the blessings that I longed for so,
                    Has passed me by;
Where'er she folds her holy wings I know
                    All tempests die;
O! Peace, my tired soul had need of thee!
Is thy sweet kiss denied alone to me?

Love, with her heated touches, passion-stirred,
                    Has passed me by.
I called, "O stay thy flight," but all unheard
                    My lonely cry:
O! Love, my tired heart had need of thee!
Is thy sweet kiss withheld alone from me?

Sleep, sister-twin of Peace, my waking eyes
                    So weary grow!
O! Love, thou wanderer from Paradise,
                    Dost thou not know
How oft my lonely heart has cried to thee?
But Thou, and Sleep, and Peace, come not to me.

'Tis morning now, yet silently I stand,
Uplift the curtain with a weary hand,
Look out while darkness overspreads the way,
         And long for day.

Calm peace is frightened with my mood to-night,
Nor visits my dull chamber with her light,
To guide my senses into her sweet rest
         And leave me blest.

Long hours since the city rocked and sung
Itself to slumber: only the stars swung
Aloft their torches into the midnight skies
         With watchful eyes.

No sound awakes; I, even, breathe no sigh,
Nor hear a single footstep passing by;
Yet I am not alone, for now I feel
         A presence steal

Within my chamber walls; I turn to see
The sweetest guest that courts humanity;
With subtle, slow enchantment draws she near,
         And Sleep is here.

What care I for the olive branch of Peace?
Kind Sleep will bring a thrice-distilled release,
Nepenthes, that alone her mystic hand
         Can understand.

And so she bends, this welcome sorceress,
To crown my fasting with her light caress.
Ah, sure my pain will vanish at the bliss
                    Of her warm kiss.

But still my duty lies in self-denial;
I must refuse sweet Sleep, although the trial
Will reawaken all my depth of pain.
                    So once again

I lift the curtain with a weary hand,
With more than sorrow, silently I stand,
Look out while darkness overspreads the way,
                    And long for day.

"Go, Sleep," I say, "before the darkness die,
To one who needs you even more than I,
For I can bear my part alone, but he
                    Has need of thee.

"His poor tired eyes in vain have sought relief,
His heart more tired still, with all its grief;
His pain is deep, while mine is vague and dim,
                    Go thou to him.

Dawn lights her candles in the East once more,
And darkness flees her chariot before;
The Lenten morning breaks with holy ray,
                    And it is day!

❦ 158

Once more adrift.
O'er dappling sea and broad lagoon,
O'er frowning cliff and yellow dune,
The long, warm lights of afternoon
   Like jewel dustings sift.

Once more awake.
I dreamed an hour of port and quay,
Of anchorage not meant for me;
The sea, the sea, the hungry sea
   Came rolling up the break.

Once more afloat.
The billows on my moorings press't,
They drove me from my moment's rest,
And now a portless sea I breast,
   And shelterless my boat.

Once more away.
The harbour lights are growing dim,
The shore is but a purple rim,
The sea outstretches grey and grim.
   Away, away, away!

Once more at sea,
The old, old sea I used to sail,
The battling tide, the blowing gale,
The waves with ceaseless under-wail
   The life that used to be.

Beyond a ridge of pine with russet tips
The west lifts to the sun her longing lips,

Her blushes stain with gold and garnet dye
The shore, the river and the wide far sky;

Like floods of wine the waters filter through
The reeds that brush our indolent canoe.

I beach the bow where sands in shadows lie;
You hold my hand a space, then speak good-bye.

Upwinds your pathway through the yellow plumes
Of goldenrod, profuse in August blooms

And o'er its tossing sprays you toss a kiss;
A moment more, and I see only this —

The idle paddle you so lately held,
The empty bow your pliant wrist propelled,

Some thistles purpling into violet,
Their blossoms with a thousand thorns afret,

And like a cobweb, shadowy and grey,
Far floats their down — far drifts my dream away.

And only where the forest fires have sped,
    Scorching relentlessly the cool north lands,
A sweet wild flower lifts its purple head,
And, like some gentle spirit sorrow-fed,
    It hides the scars with almost human hands.

And only to the heart that knows of grief,
    Of desolating fire, of human pain,
There comes some purifying sweet belief,
Some fellow-feeling beautiful, if brief.
    And life revives, and blossoms once again.

Know by the thread of music woven through
This fragile web of cadences I spin,
That I have only caught these songs since you
Voiced them upon your haunting violin.

The Overture

October's orchestra plays softly on
The northern forest with its thousand strings,
And Autumn, the conductor wields anon
The Golden-rod — The baton that he swings.

The Firs

There is a lonely minor chord that sings
Faintly and far along the forest ways,
When the firs finger faintly on the strings
Of that rare violin the night wind plays,
Just as it whispered once to you and me
Beneath the English pines beyond the sea.

Mosses

The lost wind wandering, forever grieves
                    Low overhead,
Above grey mosses whispering of leaves
                    Fallen and dead.
And through the lonely night sweeps their refrain
Like Chopin's prelude, sobbing 'neath the rain.

The Vine

The wild grape mantling the trail and tree,
Festoons in graceful veils its drapery,
Its tendrils cling, as clings the memory stirred
By some evasive haunting tune, twice heard.

The Maple

I

It is the blood-hued maple straight and strong,
Voicing abroad its patriotic song.

II

Its daring colours bravely flinging forth
The ensign of the Nation of the North.

Hare-Bell

Elfin bell in azure dress,
Chiming all day long,
Ringing through the wilderness
Dulcet notes of song.
Daintiest of forest flowers
Weaving like a spell —
Music through the Autumn hours,
Little Elfin bell.

The Giant Oak

And then the sound of marching armies 'woke
Amid the branches of the soldier oak,
And tempests ceased their warring cry, and dumb
The lashing storms that mettered, overcome,
Chocked by the heralding of battle smoke,
When these gnarled branches beat their martial drum.

Aspens

A sweet high treble threads its silvery song,
Voice of the restless aspen, fine and thin
It trills its pure soprano, light and long —
Like the vibretto of a mandolin.

Finale

The cedar trees have sung their vesper hymn,
And now the music sleeps —
Its benediction falling where the dim
Dusk of the forest creeps.
Mute grows the great concerto — and the light
Of day is darkening, Good-night, Good-night.
But through the night time I shall hear within
The murmur of these trees,
The calling of your distant violin
Sobbing across the seas,
And waking wind, and star-reflected light
Shall voice my answering. Good-night, Good-night.

But through the night time I shall hear within
The murmur of these trees,
The calling of your distant violin
Sobbing across the seas,
And waking wind, and star-reflected light
Shall voice my answering. Good-night, Good-night.

You are belted with gold, little brother of mine,
        Yellow gold, like the sun
That spills in the west, as a chalice of wine
        When feasting is done.

You are gossamer-winged, little brother of mine,
        Tissue winged like the mist
That broods where the marshes melt into a line
        Of vapour sun-kissed.

You are laden with sweets, little brother of mine,
        Flower sweets, like the touch
Of hands we have longed for, of arms that entwine,
        Of lips that love much.

You are better than I, little brother of mine,
        Than I, human-souled,
For you bring from the blossoms and red summer shine,
        For others, your gold.

Love, was it yesternoon, or years agone,
        You took in yours my hands,
And placed me close beside you on the throne
        Of Oriental lands?

The truant hour came back at dawn to-day,
        Across the hemispheres,
And bade my sleeping soul retrace its way
        These many hundred years.

And all my wild young life returned, and ceased
        The years that lie between,
When you were King of Egypt, and The East,
        And I was Egypt's queen.

I feel again the lengths of silken gossamer enfold
My body and my limbs in robes of emerald and gold.
I feel the heavy sunshine, and the weight of languid
                    heat
That crowned the day you laid the royal jewels at
                    my feet.

You wound my throat with hyacinths, green and
                    glist'ning serpent-wise,
My hot, dark throat that pulsed beneath the ardour
                    of your eyes;
And centuries have failed to cool the memory of
                    your hands
That bound about my arms those massive, pliant
                    golden bands.

You wreathed around my wrists long ropes of coral
and of jade,
And beaten gold that clung like coils of kisses love-
inlaid;
About my naked ankles tawny topaz chains you
wound,
With clasps of carven onyx, ruby-rimmed and golden
bound.

But not for me the Royal Pearls to bind about my
hair,
"Pearls were too passionless," you said, for one like
me to wear,
I must have all the splendour, all the jewels warm
as wine,
But pearls so pale and cold were meant for other
flesh than mine.

But all the blood-warm beauty of the gems you
thought my due
Were pallid as a pearl beside the love I gave to you;
O! Love of mine come back across the years that
lie between,
When you were King of Egypt — Dear, and I was
Egypt's Queen.

Measures of oil for others,
    Oil and red wine,
Lips laugh and drink, but never
    Are the lips mine.

Worlds at the feet of others,
    Power gods have known,
Hearts for the favoured round me
    Mine beats, alone.

Fame offering to others
    Chaplets of bays,
I with no crown of laurels.
    Only grey days.

Sweet human love for others,
    Deep as the sea,
God-sent unto my neighbour —
    But not to me.

Sometime I'll wrest from others
    More than all this,
I shall demand from Heaven
    Far sweeter bliss.

What profit then to others,
    Laughter and wine?
I'll have what most they covet —
    Death, will be mine.

Nature has wept today her pent-up grief
In tears, still trembling on the lily bell.
Remorseless raindrops fleck its bending leaf
And crystallize its yellow coronal.

And from the pansy 'neath the almond tree
The purple velvet bloom is dashed away.
The skies are lowering down so heavily,
Nature is sadder than a sigh today.

Something has hurt your heart and made you grieve.
The day has been too dark without the sun.
Something has proved too hard, but I believe
Others have suffered just as you have done.

Someone has wept today, disconsolate;
In unison with earth has nursed his pain,
And felt the world as harsh and desolate
As the dark mournful skies and chilling rain.

Someone has asked today, and been denied,
And in response sent up that saddened cry
That marks some human wish ungratified
Until their listless hopes, all sickened, die.

Someone is sad tonight, uncomforted.
The heart with all its dismal woes depressed.
A word, perhaps, they fain had left unsaid
Is burning still within that aching breast.

Someone is tired tonight, too tired to speak
Of all the hardships of the dark hour past.
Poor heart and hand have grown so slow and weak
In struggling for the well-won rest at last.

And you are tired tonight, too tired to know
The clouds have clustered in a crimson drift,
Too tired to see aloft, God's signet bow,
And o'er its joyous arch — an azure rift.

❧ AND HE SAID, FIGHT ON
(Tennyson)

Time and its ally, Dark Disarmament,
⠀⠀⠀⠀⠀⠀Have compassed me about,
Have massed their armies, and on battle bent
⠀⠀⠀⠀⠀⠀My forces put to rout;
But though I fight alone, and fall, and die,
⠀⠀⠀⠀⠀⠀Talk terms of Peace? Not I.

They war upon my fortress, and their guns
⠀⠀⠀⠀⠀⠀Are shattering its walls;
My army plays the cowards' part, and runs,
⠀⠀⠀⠀⠀⠀Pierced by a thousand balls;
They call for my surrender. I reply
⠀⠀⠀⠀⠀⠀"Give quarter now? Not I."

They've shot my flag to ribbons, but in rents
⠀⠀⠀⠀⠀⠀It floats above the height;
Their ensign shall not crown my battlements
⠀⠀⠀⠀⠀⠀While I can stand and fight.
I fling defiance at them as I cry,
⠀⠀⠀⠀⠀⠀"Capitulate? Not I."

Something so tender fills the air today.
What it may be or mean no voice can say
But all the harsh, hard things seem far away.

Something so restful lies on lake and shore.
The world seems anchored, and life's petty war
Of haste and labour gone for evermore.

Something so holy lies upon the land,
Like to a blessing from some saintly hand,
A peace we feel, though cannot understand.

Sounds of the seas grow fainter,
   Sounds of the sands have sped;
The sweep of gales,
The far white sails,
   Are silent, spent and dead.

Sounds of the days of summer
   Murmur and die away,
And distance hides
The long, low tides,
   As night shuts out the day.

❧ PROSE

The Story of a
Life of Unusual Experiences

First published in *The Moccasin Maker*,
a collection of Miss Johnson's short stories
issued by Briggs of Toronto, 1913

PART ONE

It was a very lonely little girl that stood on the deck of a huge sailing vessel while the shores of England slipped down into the horizon and the great, grey Atlantic yawned desolately westward. She was leaving so much behind her, taking so little with her, for the child was grave and old even at the age of eight, and realized that this day meant the updragging of all the tiny roots that clung to the home soil of the older land. Her father was taking his wife and family, his household goods, his fortune and his future to America, which, in the days of 1829, was indeed a venturesome step, for America was regarded as remote as the North Pole, and good-byes were, alas! very real good-byes, when travellers set sail for the New World in those times before steam and telegraph brought the two continents hand almost touching hand.

So little Lydia Bestman stood drearily watching with sorrow-filled eyes the England of her babyhood fade slowly into the distance — eyes that were fated never to see again the royal old land of her birth. Already the deepest grief that life could hold had touched her young heart. She had lost her own gentle, London-bred mother when she was but two years old. Her father had married again, and on her sixth birthday little Lydia, the youngest of a large family, had been sent away to boarding-school with an elder sister, and her home knew her no more. She was taken from school to the sailing ship; little stepbrothers and sisters had arrived and she was no longer the baby. Years afterwards she told her own little children that her one vivid recollection of England was the exquisite music of the church chimes as the ship weighed anchor in Bristol harbor — chimes that were ringing for evensong from the towers of the quaint old English churches. Thirteen weeks later that sailing vessel entered New York harbor, and life in the New World began.

Like most transplanted Englishmen, Mr Bestman cut himself completely off from the land of his fathers; his interests and his friends henceforth were all in the country of his adoption, and he chose Ohio as a site for his new home. He was a man of vast peculiarities, prejudices and extreme ideas — a man of contradictions so glaring that even his own children never understood him. He was a very narrow religionist, of the type that say many prayers and quote much Scripture, but he beat his children — both girls and boys — so severely that outsiders were at times compelled to interfere. For years these unfortunate children carried the scars left on their backs by the thongs of cat-o'-nine-tails when he punished them for some slight misdemeanor. They were all terrified at him, all obeyed him like soldiers, but none escaped his severity. The two elder ones, a boy and a girl, had married before they left England. The next girl married in Ohio, and the boys drifted away, glad to escape from a parental tyranny that made home anything but a desirable abiding-place. Finally but two remained of the first family — Lydia and her sister Elizabeth, a most loveable girl of seventeen, whose beauty of character and self-sacrificing heart made the one bright memory that remained with there scattered fledglings throughout their entire lives.

The lady who occupied the undesirable position of step-mother to these unfortunate children was of the very cold and chilling type of Englishwoman, more frequently met with two generations ago than in this age. She simply let her husband's first family alone. She took no interest in them, neglected them absolutely, but in her neglect was far kinder and more humane than their own father. Yet she saw that all the money, all the pretty clothes, all the dainties, went to her own children.

Perhaps the reader will think these unpleasant character-istics of a harsh father and a self-centred stepmother might better be omitted from this narrative, particularly as death claimed these two many years ago; but in the light of after events, it is necessary to reveal what the home environment of these children had been, how little of companionship or kindness or spoken love had entered their baby lives. The absence of mother kisses, or father comradeship, of endeavor to understand them individually, to probe their separate and various dispositions — things so essential to the development of all that is best in a child — went far towards governing their later actions in life. It drove the unselfish, sweet-hearted Elizabeth to a loveless marriage; it flung poor, little, love-hungry Lydia into alien but, fortunately, loyal and noble arms. Outsiders said, "What strange marriages!" But Lydia, at least, married where the first real kindness she had ever known called to her, and not one day of regret for that mar-riage ever entered into her life.

It came about so strangely, so inevitably, from such a tiny source, that it is almost incredible.

One day the stepmother, contrary to her usual custom, went into the kitchen and baked a number of little cakelets, probably what we would call cookies. For what sinister reason

❦ 179

no one could divine, but she counted these cakes as she took them from the baking-pans and placed them in the pantry. There were forty-nine, all told. That evening she counted them again; there were forty-eight. Then she complained to her husband that one of the children had evidently stolen a cake. (In her mind the two negro servants employed in the house did not merit the suspicion.) Mr Bestman inquired which child was fond of the cakes. Mrs. Bestman replied that she did not know, unless it was Lydia, who always liked them.

Lydia was called. Her father, frowning asked if she had taken the cake. The child said no.

"You are not telling the truth," Mr Bestman shouted, as the poor little downtrodden girl stood half terrified, consequently half guilty-mannered, before him.

"But I am truthful," she said. "I know nothing of the cake."

"You are not truthful. You stole it — you know you did. You shall be punished for this falsehood," he stormed, and reached for the cat-o'-nine tails.

The child was beaten brutally and sent to her room until she could tell the truth. When she was released she still held that she had not taken the cooky. Another beating followed, then a third, when finally the stepmother interfered and said magnanimously:

"Don't whip her any more; she has been punished enough." And once during one of the beatings she protested, saying, "Don't strike the child *on the head* that way."

But the iron had entered in Lydia's sister's soul. The injustice of it all drove gentle Elizabeth's gentleness to the winds.

"Liddy darling," she said, taking the thirteen-year-old girl-child into her strong young arms, "I know truth when I hear it. *You* never stole that cake."

"I didn't," sobbed the child, "I didn't."

❦ 180

"And you have been beaten three times for it!" And the sweet young mouth hardened into lines that were far too severe for a girl of seventeen. Then: "Liddy, do you know that Mr Evans has asked me to marry him?"

"Mr Evans!" exclaimed the child. "Why, you can't marry *him*, 'Liza! He's so ever old, and he lives away up in Canada, among the Indians."

"That's one of the reasons that I should like to marry him," said Elizabeth, her young eyes starry with zeal. "I want to work among the Indians, to help in Christianizing them, to — oh! just to help."

"But Mr Evans is so *old*," reiterated Lydia.

"Only thirty," answered the sister; "and he is such a splendid missionary, dear."

Love? No one talked of love in that household except the contradictory father, who continually talked of the love of God, but forgot to reflect that love towards his own children.

Human love was considered a non-essential in that family. Beautiful-spirited Elizabeth had hardly heard the word. Even Mr Evans had not made use of it. He had selected her as his wife more for her loveliness of character than from any personal attraction, and she in her untaught woman-hood married him, more for the reason that she desired to be a laborer in Christ's vineyard than because of any wish to be the wife of this one man.

But after the marriage ceremony, this gentle girl looked boldly into her father's eyes and said:

"I am going to take Liddy with me into the wilds of Canada."

"Well, well, well!" said her father, English-fashion. "If she wants to go, she may."

Go? The child fairly clung to the fingers of this savior-sister — the poor, little, inexperienced, seventeen-year-old bride who was giving up her youth and her girlhood to lay it

❦ 181

all upon the shrine of endeavor to bring the radiance of the Star that shone above Bethlehem to reflect its glories upon a forest-bred people of the North!

It was a long, strange journey that the bride and her little sister took. A stage coach conveyed them from their home in Ohio to Erie, Pennsylvania, where they went aboard a sailing vessel bound for Buffalo. There they crossed the Niagara River, and at Chippewa, on the Canadian side, again took a stage coach for the village of Brantford, sixty miles west.

At this place they remained over night, and the following day Mr Evans' own conveyance arrived to fetch them to the Indian Reserve, ten miles to the south-east.

In after years little Lydia used to tell that during that entire drive she thought she was going through an English avenue leading to some great estate, for the trees crowded up close to the roadways on either side, giant forest trees — gnarled oaks, singing firs, jaunty maples, graceful elms — all stretching their branches overhead. But the "avenue" seemed endless. "When do we come to the house?" she asked, innocently. "This lane is very long."

But it was three hours, over a rough corduroy road, before the little white frame parsonage lifted its roof through the forest, its broad verandahs and green outside shutters welcoming the travellers with an atmosphere of home at last.

As the horses drew up before the porch the great front door was noiselessly opened and a lad of seventeen, lithe, clean-limbed, erect, copper-coloured, ran swiftly down the steps, lifted his hat, smiled, and assisted the ladies to alight. The boy was Indian to the finger-tips, with that peculiar native polish and courtesy, that absolute ease of manner and direction of glance, possessed only by the old-fashioned type of red man of this continent. The missionary introduced him as "My young friend, the church interpreter, Mr George

Mansion, who is one of our household." (Mansion, or "Grand Mansion," is the English meaning of this young Mohawk's native name.)

The entire personality of the missionary seemed to undergo a change as his eyes rested on this youth. His hitherto rather stilted manner relaxed, his eyes softened and glowed, he invited confidence rather than repelled it; truly his heart was bound up with these forest people; he fairly exhaled love for them with every breath. He was a man of marked shyness, and these silent Indians made him forget this peculiarity of which he was sorrowfully conscious. It was probably this shyness that caused him to open the door and turn to his young wife with the ill-selected remark: "Welcome home, madam."

Madam! The little bride was chilled to the heart with the austere word. She hurried within, followed by her wondering child-sister, as soon as possible sought her room, then gave way to a storm of tears.

"Don't mind me, Liddy," she sobbed. "There's nothing wrong; we'll be happy enough here, only I think I looked for a little — petting."

With a wisdom beyond her years, Lydia did not reply, but went to the window and gazed absently at the tiny patch of flowers beyond the door — the two lilac trees in full blossom, the thread of glistening river, and behind it all, the northern wilderness. Just below the window stood the missionary and the Indian boy talking eagerly.

"Isn't George Mansion *splendid*!" said the child.

"You must call him Mr Mansion; be very careful about the *Mister*, Liddy dear," said her sister, rising and drying her eyes bravely. "I have always heard that the Indians treat one just as they are treated by one. Respect Mr Mansion, treat him as you would treat a city gentleman. Be sure he will gauge his

❦ 183

deportment by ours. Yes, dear, he *is* splendid. I like him already."

"Yes, 'Liza, so do I, and he *is* a gentleman. He looks it and acts it. I believe he *thinks* gentlemanly things."

Elizabeth laughed. "You dear little soul!" she said. "I know what you mean, and I agree with you."

That laugh was all that Lydia wanted to hear in this world, and presently the two sisters, with arms entwined, descended the stairway and joined in the conversation between Mr Evans and young George Mansion.

"Mrs. Evans," said the boy, addressing her directly for the first time. "I hoped you were fond of game. Yesterday I hunted; it was partridge I got, and one fine deer. Will you offer me the compliment of having some for dinner tonight?"

His voice was low and very distinct, his accent and expressions very marked as a foreigner to the tongue, but his English was perfect.

"Indeed I shall, Mr Mansion," smiled the girl-bride, "but I'm afraid that I don't know how to cook it."

"We have an excellent cook," said Mr Evans. "She has been with George and me ever since I came here. George is a splendid shot, and keeps her busy getting us game suppers."

Meanwhile Lydia had been observing the boy. She had never seen an Indian, consequently was trying to reform her ideas regarding them. She had not expected to see anything like this self-poised, scrupulously-dressed, fine-featured, dark stripling. She thought Indians wore savage-looking clothes, had fierce eyes and stern, set mouths. This boy's eyes were narrow and shrewd, but warm and kindly, his lips were like a Cupid's bow, his hands were narrower, smaller, than her own, but the firmness of those slim fingers, the power in those small palms, as he had helped her from the carriage, remained with her through all the years to come.

That evening at supper she noted his table deportment; it was correct in every detail. He ate leisurely, silently, gracefully; his knife and fork never clattered, his elbows never were in evidence, he made use of the right plates, spoons, forks, knives; he bore an ease, an unconsciousness of manner, that amazed her. The missionary himself was a stiff man, and his very shyness made him angular. Against such a setting young Mansion gleamed like a brown gem.

❦

For seven years life rolled slowly by. At times Lydia went to visit her two other married sisters, sometimes she remained for weeks with a married brother, and at rare intervals made brief trips to her father's house; but she never received a penny from her strange parent, and knew of but one home which was worthy the name. That was in the Canadian wilderness where the Indian Mission held out its arms to her, and the beloved sister made her more welcome than words could imply. Four pretty children had come to grace this forest household, where young George Mansion, still the veriest right hand of the missionary, had grown into a magnificent type of Mohawk manhood. These years had brought him much, and he had accomplished far more than idle chance could ever throw in his way. He had saved his salary that he earned as interpreter in the church, and had purchased some desirable property, a beautiful estate of two hundred acres, upon which he some day hoped to build a home. He had mastered six Indian languages, which, with his knowledge of English and his wonderful fluency in his own tribal Mohawk, gave him command of eight tongues, an advantage which soon brought him the position of Government interpreter in the Council of the great "Six Nations," composing the Iroquois race. Added to this, through the death of an uncle he came into the younger title of his family, which boasted blood of two noble lines. His father, speaker of the Council, held the elder title, but that did not lessen the importance of young George's title of chief.

Lydia never forgot the first time she saw him robed in the full costume of his office. Hitherto she had regarded him through all her comings and goings as her playmate, friend and boon companion; he had been to her something that had never before entered her life — he had brought warmth, kindness, fellowship and a peculiar confidential humanity that had been entirely lacking in the chill English home of her childhood. But this day, as he stood beside his veteran father, ready to take his place among the chiefs of the Grand Council, she saw revealed another phase of his life and character; she saw that he was destined to be a man among men, and for the first time she realized that her boy companion had gone a little beyond her, perhaps a little above her. They were a strange pair as they stood somewhat apart, unconscious of the picture they made. She, a gentleborn, fair English girl of twenty, her simple blue muslin frock vying with her eyes in color. He, tawny skinned, lithe, straight as an arrow, the royal blood of generations of chiefs and warriors pulsing through his arteries, his clinging buckskin tunic and leggings fringed and embroidered with countless quills, and endless stitches of colored moosehair. From his small, neat moccasins to his jet black hair tipped with an eagle plume he was every inch a man, a gentleman, a warrior.

But he was approaching her with the same ease with which he wore his ordinary "white" clothes — garments, whether buckskin or broadcloth, seemed to make but slight impression on him.

"Miss Bestman," he said, "I should like you to meet my mother and father. They are here, and are old friends of your sister and Mr Evans. My mother does not speak the English, but she knows you are my friend."

And presently Lydia found herself shaking hands with the elder chief, speaker of the council, who spoke English rather well, and with a little dark woman folded within a "broadcloth" and wearing the leggings, moccasins and short dress of her people. A curious feeling of shyness overcame the girl as her hand met that of George Mansion's mother, who herself was the most retiring, most thoroughly old-fashioned woman of her tribe. But Lydia felt that she was in the presence of one whom the young chief held far and away as above himself, as above her, as the best and greatest woman of his world; his very manner revealed it, and Lydia honored him within her heart at that moment more than she had ever done before.

But Chief George Mansion's mother, small and silent through long habit and custom, had acquired a certain masterful dignity of her own, for within her slender brown fingers she held a power that no man of her nation could wrest from her. She was "Chief Matron" of her entire blood relations, and commanded the enviable position of being the one and only person, man or woman, who could appoint a chief to fill the vacancy of one of the great Mohawk law-makers whose seat in Council had been left vacant when the voice of the Great Spirit called him to the happy hunting grounds. Lydia had heard of this national honor which was the right and title of this frail little moccasined Indian woman with whom she was shaking hands, and the thought flashed rapidly through her girlish mind: "Suppose some *one* lady in England had the marvellous power of appointing who the member should be in the British House of Lords or Commons. *Wouldn't* Great Britain honor and tremble before her?"

And here was Chief George Mansion's silent, unpretentious little mother possessing all this power among her people, and she, Lydia Bestman, shaking hands with her! It seemed very marvellous.

But that night the power of this same slender Indian mother was brought vividly before her when, unintentionally, she overheard young George say to the missionary:

"I almost lost my new title to-day, after you and the ladies had left the Council."

"Why, George boy!" exclaimed Mr Evans. "What have you done?"

"Nothing, it seems, except to be successful. The Council objected to my holding the title of chief and having a chief's vote in the affairs of the people, and at the same time being Government interpreter. They said it would give me too much power to retain both positions. I must give up one—my title or my Government position."

"What did you do?" demanded Mr Evans, eagerly.

"Nothing, again," smiled the young chief. "But my mother did something. She took the floor of the Council, and spoke for forty minutes. She said I must hold the position of chief which she had made for me, as well as of interpreter which I had made for myself; that if the Council objected, she would forever annul the chief's title in her own family; she would never appoint one in my place, and that we proud, arrogant Mohawks would then have only eight representatives in Council—only be on a level with, as she expressed it, 'those dogs of Senecas.' Then she clutched her broadcloth about her, turned her back on us all, and left the Council."

"What did the Council do?" gasped Mr Evans.

"Accepted me as chief and interpreter," replied the young man, smiling, "There was nothing else to do."

"Oh, you royal woman! You loyal, loyal mother!" cried Lydia to herself. "How I love you for it!"

Then she crept away just as Mr Evans had sprung forward with both hands extended towards the young chief, his

❦ 188

eyes beaming with almost fatherly delight.

Unconsciously to herself, the English girl's interest in the young chief had grown rapidly year after year. She was also unconscious of his aim at constant companionship with herself. His devotion to her sister, whose delicate health alarmed them all, more and more, as time went on, was only another royal road to Lydia's heart. Elizabeth was becoming frail, shadowy, her appetite was fitful, her eyes larger and more wistful, her fingers smaller and weaker. No one seemed to realize the insidious oncreeping of "the white man's disease," consumption, that was paling Elizabeth's fine English skin, heightening her glorious English color, sapping her delicate English veins. Only young George would tell himself over and over: "Mrs. Evans is going away from us some day, and Lydia will be left with no one in the world but me—no one but me to understand — or to — care."

So he scoured the forest for dainties, wild fruits, game, flowers, to tempt the appetite and the eye of the fading wife of the man who had taught him all the English and the white man's etiquette that he had ever mastered. Night after night he would return from day-long hunting trips, his game-bag filled with delicate quail, rare woodcock, snowy-breasted partridge, and when the illusive appetite of the sick woman could be coaxed to partake of a morsel, he felt repaid for miles of tramping through forest trails, for hours of search and skill.

PART TWO

Perhaps it was this grey shadow stealing on the forest mission, the thought of the day when that beautiful mothering sister would leave his little friend Lydia alone with a bereft man and four small children, or perhaps it was a yet more personal note in his life that brought George

Mansion to the realization of what this girl had grown to be to him.

Indian-wise, his parents had arranged a suitable marriage for him, selecting a girl of his own tribe, of the correct clan to mate with his own, so that the line of blood heritage would be intact, and the sons of the next generation would be of the "Blood Royal," qualified by rightful lineage to inherit the title of chief.

This Mohawk girl was attractive, young, and had a partial English education. Her parents were fairly prosperous, owners of many acres, and much forest and timber country. The arrangement was regarded as an ideal one — the young people as perfectly and diplomatically mated as it was possible to be; but when his parents approached the young chief with the proposition, he met it with instant refusal.

"My father, my mother," he begged, "I ask you to forgive me this one disobedience. I ask you to forgive that I have, amid my fight and struggle for English education, forgotten a single custom of my people. I have tried to honor all the ancient rules and usages of my forefathers, but I forgot this one thing, and I cannot, cannot do it! My wife I must choose for myself."

"You will marry — whom, then?" asked the chief.

"I have given no thought to it — yet," he faltered.

"Yes," said his mother, urged by the knowing heart of a woman, "yes, George, you have thought of it."

"Only this hour," he answered, looking directly into his mother's eyes. 'Only now that I see you want me to give my life to someone else. But my life belongs to the white girl, Mrs. Evans' sister, if she will take it. I shall offer it to her to-morrow — to-day."

His mother's face took on the shadow of age. "You would marry a *white* girl?" she exclaimed, incredulously.

"Yes," came the reply, briefly, decidedly.

"But your children, your sons and hers — they could never hold the title, never be chief," she said, rising to her feet.

He winced. "I know it. I had not thought of it before— but I know it. Still, I would marry her."

"But there would be no more chiefs of the Grand Mansion name," cut in his father. "The title would go to your aunt's sons. She is a Grand Mansion no longer; she, being married, is merely a Straight-Shot, her husband's name. The Straight-Shots never had noble blood, never wore a title. Shall our family title go to a *Straight-Shot?*" and the elder chief mouthed the name contemptuously.

Again the boy winced. The hurt of it all was sinking in — he hated the Straight-Shots, he loved his own blood and bone. With lightning rapidity he weighed it all mentally, then spoke: "Perhaps the white girl will not marry me," he said slowly, and the thought of it drove the dark red from his cheeks, drove his finger-nails into his palms.

"Then, then you will marry Dawendine, our choice?" cried his mother, hopefully.

"I shall marry no one but the white girl," he answered, with set lips. "If she will not marry me, I shall never marry, so the Straight-Shots will have our title, anyway."

The door closed behind him. It was as if it had shut forever between him and his own.

But even with this threatened calamity looming before her, the old Indian mother's hurt heart swelled with a certain pride in his wilful actions.

"What bravery!" she exclaimed. "What courage to hold to his own choice! What a *man!*"

"Yes," half bemoaned his father, "he is a red man through and through. He defies his whole nation in his fearlessness, his lawlessness. Even I bow to his bravery, his self-will, but that bravery is hurting me here, here!" and the ancient chief laid his hand above his heart.

❧ 191

There was no reply to be made by the proud though pained mother. She folded her "broadcloth" about her, filled her small carven pipe and sat for many hours smoking silently, silently, silently. Now and again she shook her head mournfully, but her dark eyes would flash at times with an emotion that contradicted her dejected attitude. It was an emotion born of self-exaltation, for had she not mothered a *man?* — albeit that manhood was revealing itself in scorning the traditions and customs of her ancient race.

And young George was returning from his father's house to the Mission with equally mixed emotions. He knew he had dealt an almost unforgivable blow to those beloved parents whom he had honored and obeyed from his baby-hood. Once he almost turned back. Then a vision arose of a fair young English girl whose unhappy childhood he had learned of years ago, a sweet, homeless face of great beauty, lips that were made for love they had never had, eyes that had already known more of tears than they should have shed in a lifetime. Suppose some other youth should win this girl away from him? Already several of the young men from the town drove over more frequently than they had cause to. Only the week before he had found her seated at the little old melodeon playing and singing a duet with one of these gallants. He locked his teeth together and strode rapidly through the forest path, with the first full realization that she was the only woman in all the world for him.

Some inevitable force seemed to be driving him towards — circumstances seemed to pave the way to — their ultimate union; even now chance placed her in the path, literally, for as he threaded his way uphill, across the open, and on to the little log bridge which crossed the ravine immediately behind the Mission, he saw her standing at the further side, leaning upon the unpeeled sapling which formed the bridge guard. She was looking into the tiny stream beneath. He made no sound as he approached. Generations of moccasin-shod ancestors had made his own movements swift and silent. Notwithstanding this, she turned, and, with a bright girlish smile, she said:

"I knew you were coming, Chief?"

"Why? How?" he asked, accepting his new title from her with a graceful indifference almost beyond his four-and-twenty years.

"I can hardly say just how — but — " she ended with only a smile. For a full minute he caught and held her glance. She seemed unable to look away, but her grave, blue English eyes were neither shy nor confident. They just seemed to answer his — then,

"Miss Bestman, will you be my wife?" he asked gently. She was neither surprised nor dismayed, only stood silent, as if she had forgotten the art of speech. "You knew I should ask this some day," he continued, rather rapidly. "This is the day."

"I did not really know — I don't know how I feel — " she began, faltering.

"I did not know how I felt, either, until an hour ago," he explained. "When my father and my mother told me they had arranged my marriage with — "

"With whom?" she almost demanded.

"A girl of my own people," he said, grudgingly. "A girl I honor and respect, but — "

"But what?" she said weakly, for the mention of his possible marriage with another had flung her own feelings into her very face.

"But unless you will be my wife, I shall never marry." He folded his arms across his chest as he said it — the very action expressed finality. For a second he stood erect, dark, slender, lithe, immovable, then with sudden impulse he held out one hand to her and spoke very quietly. "I love you, Lydia. Will you come to me?"

"Yes," she answered clearly. "I will come."

He caught her hands very tightly, bending his head until his fine face rested against her hair. She knew then that she had loved him through all these years, and that come what might, she would love him through all the years to be.

That night she told her frail and fading sister, whom she found resting among her pillows.

"'Liza dear, you are crying," she half sobbed in alarm, as the great tears rolled slowly down the wan cheeks. "I have made you unhappy, and you are ill, too. Oh, how selfish I am! I did not think that perhaps it might distress you."

"Liddy, Liddy darling, these are the only tears of joy that I have ever shed!" cried Elizabeth. "Joy, joy, girlie! I have so wished this to come before I left you, wished it for years. I love George Mansion better than I ever loved brother of mine. Of all the world I should have chosen him for your husband. Oh! I am happy, happy, child, and you will be happy with him, too."

And that night Lydia Bestman laid her down to rest, with her heart knowing the greatest human love that had ever entered into her life.

Mr. Evans was almost beside himself with joyousness when the young people rather shyly confessed their engagement to him. He was deeply attached to his wife's young sister, and George Mansion had been more to him than many a man's son ever is. Seemingly cold and undemonstrative, this reserved Scotch missionary had given all his heart and life to the Indians, and this one boy was the apple of his eye. Far-sighted and cautious, he saw endless trouble shadowing the young lovers—opposition to the marriage from both sides of the house. He could already see Lydia's family smarting under the seeming disgrace of her marriage to an Indian; he could see George's family indignant and hurt to the core at his marriage with a white girl; he could see how impossible it would be for Lydia's people to ever understand the fierce resentment of the Indian parents that the family title could never continue under the family name. He could see how little George's people would ever understand the "white" prejudice against them. But the good man kept his own counsel, determining only that when the war did break out, he would stand shoulder to shoulder with these young lovers and be their friend and helper when even their own blood and kin should cut them off.

It was two years before this shy and taciturn man fully realized what the young chief and the English girl really were to him, for affliction had laid a heavy hand on his heart. First, his gentle and angel-natured wife said her long, last good-night to him. Then an unrelenting scourge of scarlet fever swept three of his children into graves. Then the eldest, just on the threshold of sweet young maidenhood, faded like a flower, until she, too, said good-night and slept beside her mother. Wifeless, childless, the stricken missionary hugged to his heart these two — George and Lydia — and they, who had labored weeks and months, night and day, nursing and tending these loved ones, who had helped fight and grapple with death five times within two years, only to be driven back heartsore and conquered by the enemy — these two put away the thought of marriage for the time. Joy would have been ill-fitting in that household. Youth was theirs, health was theirs, and duty also was theirs — duty to this man of God, whose house was their home, whose hand had brought them together. So the marriage did not take place at once, but the young chief began making preparations on the estate he had purchased to build a fitting home for this homeless girl who was giving her life into his hands. After so many dark days, it was a relief to get Mr. Evans interested in the plans of the house George was to build, to select the proper situation, to arrange for a barn, a carriage house, a stable, for young Mansion had saved money and acquired property of sufficient value to give his wife a home that would vie with anything in the large border towns. Like most Indians, he was recklessly extravagant, and many a time the thrifty Scotch blood of the missionary would urge more economy, less expenditure. But the building went on; George determined it was to be a "Grand Mansion." His very title demanded that he give his wife an abode worthy of the ancestors who appropriated the name as their own.

"When you both go from me, even if it is only across the fields to the new home, I shall be very much alone," Mr. Evans had once said. Then in an agony of fear that his solitary life would shadow their happiness, he added quickly, "But I have a very sweet and lovely niece who writes me she will come to look after this desolated home if I wish it, and perhaps her brother will come, too, if I want him. I am afraid I *shall* want him sorely, George. For though you will be but five minutes' walk from me, your face will not be at my breakfast table to help me begin each day with a courage it has always inspired. So I beg that you two will not delay your marriage; give no thought to me. You are young but once, and youth has wings of wonderful swiftness. Margaret and Christopher shall come to me; but although they are my own flesh and blood, they will never become to me what you two have been, and always will be."

Within their recollection, the lovers had never heard the missionary make so long a speech. They felt the earnestness of it, the truth of it, and arranged to be married when the golden days of August came. Lydia was to go to her married sister, in the eastern part of Canada, whose husband was a clergyman, and at whose home she had spent many of her girlhood years. George was to follow. They were to be quietly married and return by sailing vessel up the lakes, then take the stage from what is now the city of Toronto, arrive at the Indian Reserve, and go direct to the handsome home the young chief had erected for his English bride. So Lydia Bestman set forth on her long journey from which she was to return as the wife of the head chief of a powerful tribe of Indians — a man revered, respected, looked up to by a vast nation, a man of sterling worth, of considerable wealth as riches were counted in those days, a man polished in the usages and etiquette of her own people, who conducted himself with faultless grace, who would have shone brilliantly in any drawing-room (and who in after years was the guest of honor at many a great reception by the governors of the land), a man young, stalwart, handsome, with an aristocratic lineage that bred him a native gentleman, with a grand old title that had come down to him through six hundred years of honor in warfare and the high places of his people. That this man should be despised by her relatives and family connections because of his warm, red skin and Indian blood, never occurred to Lydia. Her angel sister had loved the youth, the old Scotch missionary little short of adored him. Why, then, this shocked amazement of her relatives, that she should wish to wed the finest gentleman she had ever met, the man whose love and kindness had made her erstwhile blackened and cruel world a paradise of sunshine and contentment? She was but little prepared for the scorn of indignation that met her announcement that she was engaged to marry a Mohawk Indian chief.

Her sister, with whom she never had anything in common, who was years older, and had been married in England when Lydia was but three years of age, implored, entreated, sneered, ridiculed and stormed. Lydia sat motionless through it all, and then the outraged sister struck a vital spot with: "I don't know what Elizabeth has been thinking of all these years, to let you associate with Indians on an equality. *She* is to blame for this."

Then, and only then, did Lydia blaze forth. "Don't you *dare* speak of 'Liza like that!" flung the girl. "She was the only human being in our whole family, the only one who ever took me in her arms, who ever called me 'dear,' who ever kissed me as if she meant it. I tell you, she loved George Mansion better than she loved her cold, chilly English brothers. She loved *me*, and her house was my home, which yours never was. Yes, she loved me, angel girl that she was, and she died in a halo of happiness because I was happy and because I was to marry the noblest, kingliest gentleman I ever met." The girl ceased, breathless.

"Yes," sneered her sister, "yes, marry an *Indian!*"

"Yes," defied Lydia, "an *Indian*, who can give me not only a better home than this threadbare parsonage of yours" — here she swept scornful eyes about the meagre little, shabby room — "yes, a home that any Bestman would be proud to own; but better than that," she continued ragingly, "he has given me love — *love*, that you in your chilly, inhuman home sneer at, but that I have cried out for; love that my dead mother prayed should come to me, from the moment she left me a baby, alone, in England, until the hour when this one splendid man took me into his heart."

"Poor mother!" sighed the sister. "I am grateful she is spared *this*."

"Don't think that she doesn't know it!" cried Lydia. "If 'Liza approved, mother does, and she is glad of her child's happiness."

"Her child — yes, her child," taunted the sister. "Child! child! Yes, and what of the *child* you will probably mother?"

❧ 198

The crimson swept painfully down the young girl's face, but she braved it out.

"Yes," she stammered, "a child, perhaps a *son*, a son of mine, who, poor boy, can never inherit his father's title."

"And why not, pray?" remarked her sister.

"Because the female line of lineage will be broken," explained the girl. "He *should* marry someone else, so that the family title could follow the family name. His father and mother have practically cast him off because of me. *Don't* you see? Can't you understand that I am only an untitled commoner to his people? I am only a white girl."

"*Only* a white girl!" repeated the sister, sarcastically. "Do you mean to tell me that you believe these wretched Indians don't want him to marry you? *You*, a *Bestman*, and an English girl? Nonsense, Lydia! You are talking utter nonsense." But the sister's voice weakened, nevertheless.

"But it's true," asserted the girl. "You don't understand the Indian nation as 'Liza did; it's perfectly true — a son of mine can claim no family title; the honor of it must leave the name of Mansion forever. Oh, his parents have completely shut him out of their lives because I am only a white girl!" and the sweet young voice trembled woefully.

"I decline to discuss this disgraceful matter with you any further," said the sister coldly. "Perhaps my good husband can bring you to your senses," and the lady left the room in a fever of indignation.

But her "good husband," the city clergyman, declined the task of "bringing Lydia to her senses." He merely sent for her to go to his study, and, as she stood timidly in the doorway, he set his small steely eyes on her and said:

"You will leave this house at once, to-night. *To-night*, do you hear? I'll have no Indian come *here* after my wife's sister. I hope you quite understand me?"

❦ 199

"Quite sir," replied the girl, and with a stiff bow she turned and went back to her room.

In the haste of packing up her poor and scanty wardrobe, she heard her sister's voice saying to the clergyman: "Oh! how *could* you send her away? You know she has no home, she has nowhere to go. How *could* you do it?" All Lydia caught of his reply was: "Not another night, not another meal, in this house while *I* am its master."

Presently her sister came upstairs carrying a plate of pudding. Her eyes were red with tears, and her hands trembled. "Do eat this, my dear; some tea is coming presently," she said.

But Lydia only shook her head, strapped her little box, and, putting on her bonnet, she commanded her voice sufficiently to say: "I am going now. I'll send for this box later."

"Where are you going to?" her sister's voice trembled.

"I — don't know," said the girl. "But wherever I go, it will be a kindlier place than this. Good-bye, sister." She kissed the distressed wife softly on each cheek, then paused at the bedroom door to say, "The man I am to marry loves me, honors me too much to treat me as a mere possession. I know that *he* will never tell me he is 'master.' George Mansion may have savage blood in his veins, but he has grasped the meaning of the word 'Christianity' far more fully than your husband has."

Her sister could not reply, but stood with streaming eyes and watched the girl slip down the back stairs and out of a side door.

For a moment Lydia Bestman stood on the pavement and glanced up and down the street. The city was what was known as a garrison town in the days when the British regular troops were quartered in Canada. Far down the street two gay young officers were walking, their brilliant uniforms making a pleasant splash of color in the sunlight. They seemed to suggest to the girl's mind a more than welcome thought. She knew the major's wife well, a gracious, whole-souled English lady whose kindness had oftentimes bright-ened her otherwise colorless life. Instinctively the girl turned to the quarters of the married officers. She found the major's wife at home, and, burying her drawn little face in the good lady's lap, she poured forth her entire story.

"My dear," blazed out the usually placid lady, "if I were only the major for a few moments, instead of his wife, I should — I should — well, I should just *swear*! There, now I've said it, and I'd *do* it, too. Why, I never heard of such an outrage! My dear, kiss me, and tell me — when how, do you expect your young chief to come for you?"

"Next week," said the girl, from the depths of those sheltering arms.

"Then here you stay, right here with me. The major and I shall go to the church with you, see you safely married, bring you and your Hiawatha home for a cosy little break-fast, put you aboard the boat for Toronto, and give you both our blessing and our love." And the major's wife nodded her head with such emphasis that her quaint English curls bobbed about, setting Lydia off into a fit of laughter. "That's right, my dear. You just begin to laugh now, and keep it up for all the days to come. I'll warrant you've had little laughter in your young life," she said knowingly. "From what I've known of your father, he never ordered laughter as a daily ingredient in his children's food. Then that sweet Elizabeth leaving you alone, so terribly alone, must have chased the sunshine far from your little world. But after this," she added brightly, "it's just going to be love and laughter. And now, my dear, we must get back the rosy English color in your cheeks, or your young Hiawatha won't know his little white sweetheart. Run away to my spare room, girlie. The orderly will get a man to fetch your box. Then you can change your

frock. Leave yesterday behind you forever. Have a little rest
you look as if you had not slept for a week. Then join th
major and me at dinner, and we'll toast you and your redski
lover in true garrison style."

And Lydia, with the glorious recuperation of youth, ra
joyously upstairs, smiling and singing like a lark, trans
formed with the first unadulterated happiness she had eve
felt or known.

PART THREE

Upon George Mansion's arrival at th
garrison town he had been met on the wharf by the majo
who took him to the hotel, while hurriedly explaining jus
why he must not go near Lydia's sister and the clergyma
whom George had expected would perform the marriag
ceremony. "So," continued the major, "you and Lydia ar
not to be married at the cathedral after all, but Mrs. Harol
and I have arranged that the ceremony shall take place a
little St. Swithin's Church in the West End. So you'll b
there at eleven o'clock, eh, boy?"

"Yes, major, I'll be there, and before eleven, I'm afraid
I'm so anxious to take her home. I shall not endeavor t
thank you and Mrs. Harold for what you have done for m
homeless girl. I can't even — "

"Tut, tut, tut!" growled the major. "Haven't done any
thing. Bless my soul, Chief, take my word for it, haven't don
a thing to be thanked for. Here's your hotel. Get some coffe
to brace your nerves up with, for I can assure you, boy,
wedding is a trying ordeal, even if there is but a handful o
folks to see it through. Be a good boy, now — good-bye unti
eleven—St. Swithin's, remember, and God bless you!" an
the big-hearted, blustering major was whisked away in hi

carriage, leaving the young Indian half overwhelmed with his kindness, but as happy as the golden day.

An hour or so later he stood at the hotel door a moment awaiting the cab that was to take him to the church. He was dressed in the height of the fashion of the early fifties — very dark wine broadcloth, the coat shaped tightly to the waist and adorned with a silk velvet collar, a pale lavender, flowered satin waistcoat, a dull white silk stock collar, a bell-shaped black silk hat. He carried his gloves, for throughout his entire life he declared he breathed through his hands, and the wearing of gloves was abhorrent to him. Suddenly a gentleman accosted him with:

"I hear an Indian chief is in town. Going to be married here this morning. Where is the ceremony to take place? Do you know anything of it?"

Like all his race, George Mansion has a subtle sense of humor. It seized upon him now.

"Certainly I know," he replied. 'I happened to come down on the boat with the chief. I intend to go to the wedding myself. I understand the ceremony was arranged to be at the cathedral."

"Splendid!" said the gentleman. "And thank you, sir."

Just then the cab arrived. Young Mansion stepped hastily in, nodded good-bye to his acquaintance, and smilingly said in an undertone to the driver, "St. Swithin's Church — and quickly."

❧

"With this ring I thee wed," he found himself saying to a little figure in a soft grey gown at his side, while a gentle-faced old clergyman in a snowy surplice stood before him, and a square-shouldered, soldierly person in a brilliant uniform almost hugged his elbow.

"I pronounce you man and wife." At the words she turned

❧ 203

towards her husband like a carrier pigeon winging for home
Then somehow the solemnity all disappeared. The major
the major's wife, two handsome young officers, one gir
friend, the clergyman, the clergyman's wife, were all em
bracing her, and she was dimpling with laughter and hap
piness; and George Mansion stood proudly by, his fine dark
face eager, tender and very noble.

"My dear," whispered the major's wife, "he's a perfec
prince—he's just as royal as he can be! I never saw such
manners, such ease. Why, girlie, he's a courtier!"

"Confound the young rogue!" growled the major, in her
ear. "I haven't an officer on my staff that can equal him
You're a lucky girl. Yes, confound him, I say!"

"Bless you, child," said the clergyman's wife. "I think he'l
make you happy. Be very sure that you make *him* happy."

And to all these whole-hearted wishes and comments
Lydia replied with smiles and carefree words. Then came the
major, watch in hand, military precision and promptitude in
his very tone.

"Time's up, everybody! There's a bite to eat at the
barracks, then these youngsters must be gone. The boat is
due at one o'clock — time's up."

As the little party drove past the cathedral they observed
a huge crowd outside, waiting for the doors to be opened
Lydia laughed like a child as George told her of his duplicity
of the morning, when he had misled the inquiring stranger
into thinking the Indian chief was to be married there. The
little tale furnished fun for all at the pretty breakfast in the
major's quarters.

"Nice way to begin your wedding morning, young man!"
scowled the major, fiercely. "Starting this great day with a
network of falsehoods."

"Not at all," smiled the Indian. "It was arranged for the
cathedral, and I did attend the ceremony."

'No excuses, you bare-faced scoundrel! I won't listen to them. Here you are happily married, and all those poor would-be sight-seers sizzling out there in this glaring August sun. I'm ashamed of you!" But his arm was about George's shoulders, and he was wringing the dark, slender hand with a genuine good fellowship that was pleasant to see. "Bless my soul, I love you, boy!" he added, sincerely. "Love you through and through; and remember, I'm your white father from this day forth."

"And I am your white mother," said the major's wife, placing her hands on his shoulders.

For a second the bridegroom's face sobered. Before him flashed a picture of a little old Indian woman with a broad-cloth folded about her shoulders, a small carven pipe between her lips, a world of sorrow in her deep eyes—sorrow that he had brought there. He bent suddenly and kissed Mrs. Harold's fingers with a grave and courtly deference. "Thank you," he said simply.

But, motherlike, she knew that his heart was bleeding. Lydia had told of his parents' antagonism, of the lost Mansion title. So the good lady just gave his hand a little extra, understanding squeeze, and the good-byes began.

"Be off with you, youngsters!" growled the major. "The boat is in — post haste now, or you'll miss it. Begone, both of you!"

And presently they found themselves once more in the carriage, the horses galloping down to the wharf. And almost before they realized it they were aboard, with the hearty "God bless you's" of the splendid old major and his lovable wife still echoing in their happy young hearts.

It was evening, five days later, when they arrived at their new home. All about the hills, and the woods, above the winding river, and along the edge of the distant forest, brooded that purple smokiness that haunts the late days of August — the smokiness that was born of distant fires, where the Indians and pioneers were "clearing" their lands. The air was like amethyst, the setting sun a fire opal. As on the day when she first had come into his life, George helped her to alight from the carriage, and they stood a moment, hand in hand, and looked over the ample acres that composed their estate. The young Indian had worked hard to have most of the land cleared, leaving here and there vast stretches of walnut groves, and long lines of majestic elms, groups of sturdy oaks, and occasionally a single regal pine tree. Many a time in later years his utilitarian friends would say, "Chief, these trees you are preserving so jealously are eating up a great deal of your land. Why not cut them away and grow wheat?" But he would always resent the suggestion, saying that his wheat lands lay back from the river. They were for his body, doubtless, but here, by the river, the trees must be — they were for his soul. And Lydia would champion him immediately with, "Yes, they were there to welcome me as a bride, those grand old trees, and they will remain there, I think, as long as we both shall live." So, that first evening at home they stood and watched the imperial trees, the long, open flats bordering the river, the nearby lawns which he had taken such pains to woo from the wilderness; stood palm to palm, and that moment seemed to govern all their after life.

Someone has said that never in the history of the world have two people been perfectly mated. However true this may be, it is an undeniable fact that between the most devoted of life-mates there will come inharmonious moments. Individuality would cease to exist were it not so. These two lived together for upwards of thirty years, and never had one single quarrel, but oddly enough, when the rare inharmonous moments came, these groups of trees bridged the fleeting difference of opinion or any slight antagonism of will and purpose; when these unresponsive moments came, one or the other would begin to admire those forest giants, to suggest improvements, to repeat the admiration of others for their graceful outlines — to, in fact, direct thought and conversation into the common channel of love for those trees. This peculiarity was noticeable to outsiders, to their own circle, to their children. At mere mention of the trees the shadow of coming cloud would lessen, then waste, then grow invisible. Their mutual love for these voiceless yet voiceful and kingly creations was as the love of children for a flower — simple, nameless, beautiful and powerful beyond words.

That first home night as she stepped within doors, there awaited two inexpressible surprises for her. First, on the dining-room table a silver tea service of seven pieces imported from England — his wedding gift to her. Second, in the quaint little drawing-room stood a piano. In the "early fifties" this latter was indeed a luxury, even in city homes. She uttered a little cry of delight, and flinging herself before the instrument, ran her fingers over the keys and broke into his favorite song, "Oft in the Stilly Night." She had a beautiful voice, the possession of which would have made her renowned had opportunity afforded its cultivation. She had "picked up" music and read it remarkably well, and he, Indian wise, was passionately fond of melody. So they laughed and loved together over this new luxurious toy, until Milly, the ancient Mohawk maid, tapped softly at the drawing-room and bade them come to tea. With the first meal in her new home, the darkened hours and days and years smothered their haunting voices. She had "left yesterday behind her," as the major's royal wife had wished her to, and for the first time in all her checkered and neglected life she laughed with the gladness of a bird at song, flung her past behind her, and the grim unhappiness of her former life left her forever.

❦

It was a golden morning in July when the doctor stood grasping George Mansion's slender hands, searching into his dusky, anxious eyes, and saying with ringing cheeriness, "Chief, I congratulate you. You've got the most beautiful son upstairs — the finest boy I ever saw. Hail to the young chief, I say!"

The doctor was white. He did not know of the broken line of lineage — that "the boy upstairs" could never wear his father's title. A swift shadow fought for a second with glorious happiness. The battlefield was George Mansion's face, his heart. His unfilled duty to his parents assailed him like a monstrous enemy, then happiness conquered, came forth a triumphant victor, and the young father dashed noiselessly, fleetly up the staircase, and, despite the protesting physician, in another moment his wife and son were in his arms. Titles did not count in that moment; only Love in its tyrannical majesty reigned in that sacred room.

The boy was a being of a new world, a new nation. Before he was two weeks old he began to show the undeniable physique of the two great races from whence he came; all the better qualities of both bloods seemed to blend within his small body. He was his father's son, he was his mother's baby. His grey-blue eyes held a hint of the dreaming forest, but also a touch of old England's skies. His hair, thick and black, was straight as his father's, except just above the temples, where a suggestion of his mother's pretty English curls waved like strands of fine silk. His small mouth was thin-lipped; his nose, which even in babyhood never had the infantile "snub," but grew straight, thin as his Indian ancestors', yet displayed a half-haughty English nostril; his straight little back — all combined likenesses to his parents. But who could say which blood dominated his tiny person? Only the exquisite soft, pale brown of his satiny skin called loudly and insistently that he was of a race older than the composite English could ever boast; it was the hallmark of his ancient heritage — the birthright of his father's son.

But the odd little half-blood was extraordinarily handsome even as an infant. In after years when he grew into glorious manhood he was generally acknowledged to be the handsomest man in the Province of Ontario — but to-day — his first day in these strange, new surroundings — he was but a wee, brown, lovable bundle, whose tiny gossamer hands cuddled into his father's palm, while his little velvet cheek lay rich and russet against the pearly whiteness of his mother's arm.

"I believe he is like you, George," she murmured, with a wealth of love in her voice and eyes.

"Yes," smiled the young chief, "he certainly has Mansion blood; but your eyes, Lydia, your dear eyes."

"Which eyes must go to sleep and rest," interrupted the physician, severely. "Come, Chief, you've seen your son, you've satisfied yourself that Mrs. Mansion is doing splendidly, so away you go, or I shall scold."

And George slipped away after one more embrace, slipped down the staircase, and out into the radiant July sunshine, where his beloved trees arose about him, grand and majestic, seeming to understand how full of joy, of exultation, had been this great new day.

The whims of women are proverbial, but the whims of men are things never to be accounted for. This beautiful child was but a few weeks old when Mr Bestman wrote, announcing to his daughter his intention of visiting her for a few days.

So he came to the Indian Reserve, to the handsome country home his Indian son-in-law had built. He was amazed, surprised, delighted. His English heart revelled in the trees. "Like an Old Country gentleman's estate in the Counties," he declared. He kissed his daughter with affection, wrung his son-in-law's hand with a warmth and cordiality unmistakable in its sincerity, took the baby in his arms and said over and over, "Oh, you sweet little child! You sweet little child!" Then the darkness of all those harsh years fell away from Lydia. She could afford to be magnanimous, so with a sweet silence, a loving forgetfulness of all the dead miseries and bygone whip-lashes, she accepted her strange parent just as he presented himself, in the guise of a man whom the years had changed from harshness to tenderness, and let herself thoroughly enjoy his visit.

But when he drove away she had but one thing to say; it was, "George, I wonder when *your* father will come to us, when your *mother* will come. Oh, I want her to see the baby, for I think my own mother sees him."

"Some day, dear," he answered hopefully. "They will come some day; and when they do, be sure it will be to take you to their hearts."

She sighed and shook her head unbelievingly. But the "some day" that he prophesied, but which she doubted, came in a manner all too soon — all too unwelcome. The little son had just begun to walk about nicely, when George Mansion was laid low with a lingering fever that he had contracted among the marshes where much of his business as an employee of the Government took him. Evils had begun to creep into his forest world. The black and subtle evil of the white man's firewater had commenced to touch with its poisonous finger the lives and lodges of his beloved people.

The curse began to spread, until it grew into a menace to the community. It was the same old story: the white man had come with the Bible in one hand, the bottle in the other. George Mansion had striven side by side with Mr Evans to overcome the dread scourge. Together they fought the enemy hand to hand, but it gained ground in spite of all their efforts. The entire plan of the white liquor dealer's campaign was simply an effort to exchange a quart of bad whiskey for a cord of first-class firewood, or timber, which could be hauled off the Indian Reserve and sold in the nearby town markets for five or six dollars; thus a hundred dollars' worth of bad whiskey, if judiciously traded, would net the white dealer a thousand dollars cash. And the traffic went on, to the depletion of the Indian forests and the degradation of the Indian souls.

Then the Canadian Government appointed young Mansion special forest warden, gave him a "VR" hammer, with which he was to stamp each and every stick of timber he could catch being hauled off the Reserve by white men; licensed him to carry firearms for self-protection, and told him to "go ahead." He "went ahead." Night after night he lay, concealing himself in the marshes, the forests, the trails, the concession lines, the river road, the Queen's highway, seizing all the timber he could, destroying all the whiskey, turning the white liquor traders off Indian lands, and fighting as only a young, earnest and inspired man can fight. These hours and conditions began to tell on his physique. The marshes breathed their miasma into his blood — the dreaded fever had him in its claws. Lydia was a born nurse. She knew little of thermometers, of charts, of technical terms, but her ability and instincts in the sick-room were unerring; and, when her husband succumbed to a raging fever, love lent her hands an inspiration and her brain a clarity that would have shamed many a professional nurse.

❦ 211

For hours, days, weeks, she waited, tended, watched, administered, labored and loved beside the sick man's bed. She neither slept nor ate enough to carry her through the ordeal, but love lent her strength, and she battled and fought for his life as only an adoring woman can. Her wonderful devotion was the common talk of the country. She saw no one save Mr Evans and the doctors. She never left the sick-room save when her baby needed her. But it all seemed so useless, so in vain, when one dark morning the doctor said, "We had better send for his father and mother."

Poor Lydia! Her heart was nearly breaking. She hurriedly told the doctor the cause that had kept them away so long, adding, "Is it so bad as that? Oh, doctor, *must I send for them*? They don't want to come." Before the good man could reply, there was a muffled knock at the door. Then Milly's old wrinkled face peered in, and Milly's voice said whisperingly, "His people — they here."

"Whose people? Who are here?" almost gasped Lydia.

"His father and his mother," answered the old woman. "They downstairs."

For a brief moment there was silence. Lydia could not trust herself to speak, but ill as he was, George's quick Indian ear had caught Milly's words. He murmured, "Mother! mother! Oh, my mother!"

"Bring her, quickly, *quickly*!" said Lydia to the doctor.

It seemed to the careworn girl that a lifetime followed before the door opened noiselessly, and there entered a slender little old Indian woman, in beaded leggings, moccasins, "short skirt," and a blue "broadcloth" folded about her shoulders. She glanced swiftly at the bed, but with the heroism of her race went first towards Lydia, laid her cheek silently beside the white girl's, then looked directly into her eyes.

"Lydia!" whispered George, "Lydia!" At the word both

women moved swiftly to his side. "Lydia," he repeated, "my mother cannot speak the English, but her cheek to yours means that you are her blood relation."

The effort of speech almost cost him a swoon, but his mother's cheek was now against his own, and the sweet, dulcet Mohawk language of his boyhood returned to his tongue; he was speaking it to his mother, speaking it lovingly, rapidly. Yet, although Lydia never understood a word, she did not feel an outsider, for the old mother's hand held her own, and she knew that at last the gulf was bridged.

❦

It was two days later, when the doctor pronounced George Mansion out of danger, that the sick man said to his wife: "Lydia, it is all over — the pain, the estrangement. My mother says that you are her daughter. My father says that you are his child. They heard of your love, your nursing, your sweetness. They want to know if you will call them 'father, mother.' They love you, for you are one of their own."

"At last, at last!" half sobbed the weary girl. "Oh, George, I am so happy! *You* are going to get well, and *they* have come to us at last."

"Yes, dear," he replied. Then with a half humorous yet wholly pathetic smile flitting across his wan face, he added, "And my mother has a little gift for you." He nodded then towards the quaint old figure at the further side of the bed. His mother arose, and, drawing from her bosom a tiny, russet-colored object, laid it in Lydia's hand. It was a little moccasin, just three and a quarter inches in length. "Its mate is lost," added the sick man, "but I wore it as a baby. My mother says it is yours, and should have been yours all these years."

For a second the two women faced each other, then Lydia sat down abruptly on the bedside, her arms slipped about the

❦ 213

older woman's shoulders, and her face dropped quickly, heavily — at last on a mother's breast.

George Mansion sighed in absolute happiness, then closed his eyes and slept the great, strong, vitalizing sleep of reviving forces.

PART FOUR

How closely the years chased one another after this! But many and many a happy day within each year found Lydia and her husband's mother sitting together, hour upon hour, needle in hand, sewing and harmonizing — the best friends in all the world. It mattered not that "mother" could not speak one word of English, or that Lydia never mastered but a half-dozen words of Mohawk. These two were friends in the sweetest sense of the word, and their lives swept forward in a unison of sympathy that was dear to the heart of the man who held them as the two most precious beings in all the world.

And with the years came new duties, new responsibilities, new little babies to love and care for, until a family, usually called "A King's Desire," gathered at their hearthside — four children, the eldest a boy, the second a girl, then another boy, then another girl. These children were reared on the strictest lines of both Indian and English principles. They were taught the legends, the traditions, the culture and the etiquette of both races to which they belonged; but above all, their mother instilled into them from the very cradle that they were of their father's people, not of hers. Her marriage had made her an Indian by the laws which govern Canada, as well as by the sympathies and yearnings and affections of her own heart. When she married George Mansion she had repeated to him the centuries-old vow of allegiance, "Thy people shall be my people, and thy God my God." She determined that should she ever be mother to his children, those children should be reared as Indians in spirit and patriotism, and in loyalty to their father's race as well as by heritage of blood. The laws of Canada held these children as Indians. They were wards of the Government; they were born on Indian lands, on Indian Reservations. They could own and hold Indian lands, and their mother, English though she was, made it her life service to inspire, foster and elaborate within these children the pride of race, the value of that copper-tinted skin which they all displayed. When people spoke of blood and lineage and nationality, these children would say, "We are Indians," with the air with which a young Spanish don might say, "I am a Castilian." She wanted them to grow up nationalists, and they did, every mother's son and daughter of them. Things could never have been otherwise, for George Mansion and his wife had so much in common that their offspring could scarcely evince other than inherited parental traits. Then tastes and distastes were so synonymous; they hated hypocrisy, vulgarity, slovenliness, imitations.

After forty years spent on a Canadian Indian Reserve, Lydia Mansion still wore real lace, real tortoise-shell combs, real furs. If she could not have procured these she would have worn plain linen collars, no combs, and a woven woolen scarf about her throat; but the imitation fabrics, as well as the "imitation people," had no more part in her life than they had in her husband's, who abhorred all such pinchbeck. Their loves were identical. They loved nature — the trees, best of all, and the river, and the birds. They loved the Anglican Church, they loved the British flag, they loved Queen Victoria, they loved beautiful, dead Elizabeth Evans, they loved strange, reticent Mr Evans. They loved music, pictures and dainty china, with which George Mansion filled his beautiful home. They loved books and animals, but, most of all, these two loved the Indian people, loved their legends, their habits, their customs — loved the people themselves. Small wonder, then, that their children should be born with pride of race and heritage, and should face the world with that peculiar, unconquerable courage that only a fighting ancestry can give.

As the years drifted on, many distinctions came to the little family of the "Grand Mansions." The chief's ability as an orator, his fluency of speech, his ceaseless war against the inroads of the border white men and their lawlessness among his own people — all gradually but surely brought him, inch by inch, before the notice of those who sat in the "seats of the mighty" of both church and state. His presence was frequently demanded at Ottawa, fighting for the cause of his people before the House of Commons, the Senate, and the Governor-General himself. At such times he would always wear his native buckskin costume, and his amazing rhetoric, augmented by the gorgeous trappings of his office and his inimitable courtesy of manner, won him friends and followers among the lawmakers of the land. He never fought for a cause and lost it, never returned to Lydia and his people except in a triumph of victory. Social honors came to him as well as political distinctions. Once, soon after his marriage, a special review of the British troops quartered at Toronto was called in his honor and he rode beside the general, making a brilliant picture, clad as he was in buckskins and scarlet blanket and astride his pet black pony, as he received the salutes of company after company of England's picked soldiers as they wheeled past. And when King Edward of England visited Canada as Prince of Wales, he fastened with his own royal hands a heavy silver medal to the buckskin covering George Mansion's breast, and the royal words were very sincere as they fell from the prince's lips: "This medal is for recognition of your loyalty in battling for your own people, even as your ancestors battled for the British Crown."

Then in later years, when Prince Arthur of Connaught accepted the title of "Chief," conferred upon him with elaborate ceremony by the chiefs, braves and warriors of the great Iroquois Council, it was George Mansion who was chosen as special escort to the royal visitor — George Mansion and his ancient and honored father, who, hand-in-hand with the young prince, walked to and fro, chanting the impressive ritual of bestowing the title. Even Bismarck, the "Iron Chancellor" of Germany, heard of this young Indian warring for the welfare of his race, and sent a few kindly words, with his own photograph, from across seas to encourage the one who was fighting, single-handed, the menace of white man's greed and white man's firewater.

And Lydia, with her glad and still girlish heart, gloried in her husband's achievements and in the recognition accorded him by the great world beyond the Indian Reserve, beyond the wilderness, beyond the threshold of their own home. In only one thing were their lives at all separated. She took no part in his public life. She hated the glare of the fierce light that beat upon prominent lives, the unrest of fame, the disquiet of public careers.

"No," she would answer, when oftentimes he begged her to accompany him and share his success and honors, "no, I was homeless so long that 'home' is now my ambition. My babies need me here, and you need me here when you return, far more than you need me on platform or parade. Go forth and fight the enemy, storm the battlements and win the laurels, but let me keep the garrison — here at home, with our babies all about me and a welcome to our warrior husband and father when he returns from war."

Then he would laugh and coax again, but always with the same result. Every day, whether he went forth to the Indian Council across the river, or when more urgent duties called him to the Capital, she always stood at the highest window waving her handkerchief until he was out of sight, and that dainty flag lent strength to his purpose and courage to his heart, for he knew the home citadel was there awaiting his return — knew that she would be at that selfsame window, their children clustered about her skirts, her welcoming hands waving a greeting instead of a good-bye, as soon as he faced the home portals once more, and in his heart of hearts George Mansion felt that his wife had chosen the wiser, greater part; that their children would some day arise and call her blessed because she refused to wing away from the home nest, even if by so doing she left him to take his flights alone.

But in all their world there was no one prouder of his laurels and successes than his home-loving little English wife, and the mother-heart of her must be forgiven for welcoming each new honor as a so much greater heritage for their children. Each distinction won by her husband only established a higher standard for their children to live up to. She prayed and hoped and prayed again that they would all be worthy such a father, that they would never fall short of his excellence. To this end she taught, labored for, and loved them, and they, in turn, child-wise, responded to her teaching, imitating her allegiance to their father, reflecting her fealty, and duplicating her actions. So she molded these little ones with the mother-hand that they felt through all their after lives, which were but images of her own in all that concerned their father.

The first great shadow that fell on this united little circle was when George Mansion's mother quietly folded her "broadcloth" about her shoulders for the last time, when the little old tobacco pipe lay unfilled and unlighted, when the finely-beaded moccasins were empty of the dear feet that had wandered so gently, so silently into the Happy Hunting Grounds. George Mansion was bowed with woe. His mother had been to him the queen of all women, and her death left a desolation in his heart that even his wife could not assuage. It was a grief he really never overcame. Fortunately his mother had grown so attached to Lydia that his one disobedience — that of his marriage — never reproached him. Had the gentle little old Indian woman died before the episode of the moccasin which brought complete reconciliation, it is doubtful if her son would ever have been quite the same again. As it was, with the silence and stoicism of his race he buried his grief in his own heart, without allowing it to cast a gloom over his immediate household.

But after that the ancient chief, his father, came more frequently to George's home, and was always an honored guest. The children loved him, Lydia had the greatest respect and affection for him, the greatest sympathy for his loneliness, and she ever made him welcome and her constant companion when he visited them. He used to talk to her much of George, and once or twice gave her grave warnings as to his recklessness and lack of caution in dealing with the ever-growing menace of the whiskey traffic among the Indians. The white men who supplied and traded this liquor were desperadoes, a lawless set of ruffians who for some time had determined to rid their stamping-ground of George Mansion, as he was the chief opponent to their business, and with the way well cleared of him and his unceasing resistance, their scoundrelly trade would be an easy matter.

"Use all your influence," the old father would say, "to urge him never to seize the ill-gotten timber or destroy their whiskey, unless he has other Indian wardens with him. They'll kill him if they can, those white men. They have been heard to threaten."

For some time this very thing had been crowding its truth about his wife's daily life. Threatening and anonymous letters had more than once been received by her husband — letters that said he would be "put out of the way" unless he stopped interfering in the liquor trade. There was no ignoring the fact that danger was growing daily, that the fervent young chief was allowing his zeal to overcome his caution, was hazarding his life for the protection of his people against a crying evil. Once a writer of these unsigned letters threatened to burn his house down in the dead of night, another to maim his horses and cattle, others to "do away" with him. His crusade was being waged under the weight of a cross that was beginning to fall on his loyal wife, and to overshadow his children. Then one night the blow fell. Blind with blood, crushed and broken, he staggered and reeled home, unaided, unassisted, and in excruciating torture. Nine white men had attacked him from behind in a border village a mile from his home, where he had gone to intercept a load of whiskey that was being hauled into the Indian Reserve. Eight of those lawbreakers circled about him, while the ninth struck him from behind with a leaden plumb attached to an elastic throw-string. The deadly thing crushed in his skull; he dropped where he stood, as if shot. Then brutal boots kicked his face, his head, his back, and, with curses, his assailants left him — for dead.

With a vitality born of generations of warriors, he regained consciousness, staggered the mile to his own gate, where he met a friend, who, with extreme concern, began to assist him into his home. But he refused the helping arm with, "No, I go alone; it would alarm Lydia if I could not walk alone." These, with the few words he spoke as he entered the kitchen, where his wife was overseeing old Milly get the evening meal, were the last intelligent words he spoke for many a day.

"Lydia, they've hurt me at last," he said, gently.

She turned at the sound of his strained voice. A thousand emotions overwhelmed her at the terrifying sight before her. Love, fear, horror, all broke forth from her lips in a sharp, hysterical cry, but above this cry sounded the gay laughter of the children who were playing in the next room, their shrill young voices raised in merriment over some new sport. In a second the mother-heart asserted itself. Their young eyes must not see this ghastly thing.

"Milly!" she cried to the devoted Indian servant, "help Chief George." Then dashing into the next room, she half sobbed, 'Children, children! hush, oh, hush! Poor father — "

She never finished the sentence. With a turn of her arm she swept them all into the drawing-room, closed the door, and flew back to her patriot husband.

For weeks and weeks he lay fighting death as only a determined man can — his upper jaw broken on both sides, his lower jaw splintered on one side, his skull so crushed that to the end of his days a silver dollar could quite easily be laid flat in the cavity, a jagged and deep hole in his back, and injuries about the knees and leg bones. And all these weeks Lydia hovered above his pillow, night and day, nursing, tending, helping, cheering. What effort it cost her to be bright and smiling no tongue can tell, for her woman's heart saw that this was but the beginning of the end. She saw it when in his delirium he raved to get better, to be allowed to get up and go on with the fight; saw that his spirit never rested, for fear that, now he was temporarily inactive, the whiskey dealers would have their way. She knew then that she must school herself to endure this thing again; that she must never ask him to give up his life work, never be less courageous than he, though that courage would mean never a peaceful moment to her when he was outside their own home.

Mr Evans was a great comfort to her during those terrible weeks. Hour after hour he would sit beside the injured man, never speaking or moving, only watching quietly, while Lydia barely snatched the necessary sleep a nurse must have, or attended to the essential needs of the children, who, however, were jealously cared for by faithful Milly. During those times the children never spoke except in whispers, their rigid Indian-English training in self-effacement and obedience being now of untold value.

But love and nursing and bravery all counted in the end, and one day George Mansion walked downstairs, the doctor's arm on one side, Lydia's on the other. He immediately asked for his pistol and his dagger, cleaned the one, oiled and sharpened the other, and said, "I'll be ready for them again in a month's time."

But while he lay injured his influential white friends and the Government at Ottawa had not been idle. The lawless creature who dealt those unmerited blows was tried, convicted and sent to Kingston Penitentiary for seven years. So one enemy was out of the way for the time being. It was at this time that advancing success lost him another antagonist, who was placed almost in the rank of an ally.

George Mansion was a guest of the bishop of his diocese, as he was a lay delegate accompanying Mr Evans to the Anglican Synod. The chief's work had reached other ears than those of the Government at Ottawa, and the bishop was making much of the patriot, when in the See House itself an old clergyman approached him with outstretched hand and the words, "I would like you to call bygones just bygones."

"I don't believe I have the honor of knowing you, sir," replied the Indian, with a puzzled but gracious look.

"I am your wife's brother-in-law," said the old clergyman, "the man who would not allow her to be married from my house — that is, married to *you*."

The Indian bit his lip and instinctively stepped backward. Added to his ancestral creed of never forgiving such injury, came a rush of memory — the backward-surging picture of his homeless little sweetheart and all that she had endured. Then came the memory of his dead mother's teaching — teaching she had learned from her own mother, and she in turn from her mother: "Always forget yourself for *old* people, always honor the *old*."

Instantly George Mansion arose — arose above the prejudices of his blood, above the traditions of his race, arose to the highest plane a man can reach — the memory of his mother's teaching.

"I would hardly be here as a lay delegate of my church were I not willing to let bygones be bygones," he said, simply, and laid his hand in that of the old clergyman, about whose eyes there was moisture, perhaps because this opportunity for peacemaking had come so tardily.

The little family of the "Grand Mansions" were now growing to very "big childhood," and the inevitable day came when Lydia's heart must bear the wrench of having her firstborn say good-bye to take his college course. She was not the type of mother who would keep the boy at home because of the heartache the good-byes must bring, but the parting was certainly a hard one, and she watched his going with a sense of loss that was almost greater than her pride in him. He had given evidence of the most remarkable musical talent. He played classical airs even before he knew a note, and both his parents were in determined unison about this talent being cultivated. The following year the oldest daughter also entered college, having had a governess at home for a year, as some preparation. But these changes brought no difference into the home, save that George Mansion's arm grew stronger daily in combat against the old foe. Then came the second attack of the enemy, when six white men beset him from behind, again knocking him insensible, with a heavy blue beech hand-spike. They broke his hand and three ribs, knocked out his teeth, injured his side and head; then, seizing his pistol, shot at him, the ball fortunately not reaching a vital spot. As his senses swam he felt them drag his poor maimed body into the middle of the road, so it would appear as if horses had trampled him, then he heard them say, "*This* time the devil is dead." But hours afterwards he again arose, again walked home, five interminable miles, again greeted his ever watchful and anxious wife with, "Lydia, they've hurt me once more." Then came weeks of renewed suffering, of renewed care and nursing, of renewed vitality, and at last of conquered health.

These two terrible illnesses seemed to raise Lydia into a peculiar, half-protecting attitude towards him. In many ways she "mothered" him almost as though he were her son — he who had always been the leader, and so strong and self-reliant. After this, when he went forth on his crusades, she watched his going with the haunting fear with which one would watch a child wandering on the edge of a chasm. She waited on him when he returned, served him with the tenderness with which one serves a cripple or a baby. Once he caught her arm, as she carried to him a cup of broth, after he had spent wearisome hours at the same old battle, and turning towards her, said softly: "You are like my mother used to be to me." She did not ask him in what way — she knew — and carried broth to him when next he came home half exhausted. Gradually he now gathered about him a little force of zealous Indians who became enthusiastic to take up arms with him against the whiskey dealers. He took greater precautions in his work, for the growing mist of haunting anxiety in Lydia's eyes began to call to him that there were

❧ 224

other claims than those of the nation. His splendid zeal had brought her many a sleepless night, when she knew he was scouring the forests for hidden supplies of the forbidden merchandise, and that a whole army of desperadoes would not deter him from fulfilling his duty of destroying it. He felt, rather than saw, that she never bade him good-bye but that she was prepared not to see him again alive. Added to this he began to suffer as she did — to find that in his good-byes was the fear of never seeing her again. He, who had always been so fearless, was now afraid of the day when he should not return and she would be once more alone.

So he let his younger and eager followers do some of the battling, though he never relaxed his vigilance, never took off his armor, so to speak. But now he spent long days and quiet nights with Lydia and his children. They entertained many guests, for the young people were vigorous and laughter-loving, and George and Lydia never grew old, never grew weary, never grew commonplace. All the year round guests came to the hospitable country house — men and women of culture, of learning, of artistic tastes, of congenial habits. Scientists, authors, artists, all made their pilgrimages to this unique household, where refinement and much luxury, and always a glad welcome from the chief and his English wife, made their visits long remembered. And in some way or other, as their children grew up, those two seemed to come closer together once more. They walked among the trees they had loved in those first bridal days, they rested by the river shore, they wandered over the broad meadows and bypaths of the old estate, they laughed together frequently like children, and always and ever talked of and acted for the good of the Indian people who were so unquestionably the greatest interest in their lives, outside their own children. But one day, when the beautiful estate he was

❦ 225

always so proud of was getting ready to smile under the suns of spring, he left her just when she needed him most, for their boys had plunged forward into the world of business in the large cities, and she wanted a strong arm to lean on. It was the only time he failed to respond to her devoted nursing, but now she could not bring him back from the river's brink, as she had so often done before. Cold had settled in all the broken places of his poor body, and he slipped away from her, a sacrifice to his fight against evil on the altar of his nation's good. In his feverish wanderings he returned to the tongue of his childhood, the beautiful, dulcet Mohawk. Then recollecting and commanding himself, he would weakly apologize to Lydia with: "I forgot; I thought it was my mother," and almost his last words were, "It must be by my mother's side," meaning his resting-place. So his valiant spirit went fearlessly forth.

❦

"Do you ever think, dear," said Lydia to her youngest child, some years later, "that you are writing the poetry that always lived in an unexpressed state here in my breast?"

"No, Marmee," answered the girl, who was beginning to mount the ladder of literature, "I never knew you wanted to *write* poetry, although I knew you loved it."

"Indeed, I did," answered the mother, "but I never could find expression for it. I was made just to sing, I often think, but I never had the courage to sing in public. But I did want to write poetry, and now you, dear, are doing it for me. How proud your father would have been of you!"

"Oh, he knows! I'm sure he knows all that I have written," answered the girl, with the sublime faith that youth has in its own convictions. "And if you like my verses, Marmee, I am sure he does, for he knows."

"Perhaps," murmured the older woman. "I often feel that

he is very near to us. I never have felt that he is really gone very far away from me."

"Poor little Marmee!" the girl would say to herself. "She misses him yet. I believe she will always miss him."

Which was the truth. She saw constantly his likeness in all her children, bits of his character, shades of his disposition, reflections of his gifts and talents, hints of his bravery, and she always spoke of these with a commending air, as though they were characteristics to be cultivated, to be valued and fostered.

At first her fear of leaving her children, even to join him, was evident, she so believed in a mother's care and love being a necessity to a child. She had sadly missed it all out of her own strange life, and she felt she *must* live until this youngest daughter grew to be a woman. Perhaps this desire, this mother-love, kept her longer beside her children than she would have stayed without it, for the years rolled on, and her hair whitened, her once springing step halted a little, the glorious blue of her English eyes grew very dreamy, and tender, and wistful. Was she seeing the great Hereafter unfold itself before her as her steps drew nearer and nearer?

And one night the Great Messenger knocked softly at her door, and with a sweet, gentle sigh she turned and followed where he led — joining gladly the father of her children in the land that holds both whites and Indians as one.

And the daughter who writes the verses her mother always felt, but found no words to express, never puts a last line to a story, or a sweet cadence into a poem, but she says to herself as she holds her mother's memory within her heart:

"She knows — she knows."

*First published Vancouver Province
September 24, 1910*

Far over your left shoulder as your boat leaves the Narrows to thread the beautiful waterways that lead to Vancouver Island, you will see the summit of Mount Baker robed in its everlasting whiteness and always reflecting some wonderful glory from the rising sun, the golden noontide, or the violet and amber sunset. This is the Mount Ararat of the Pacific Coast people. Those readers who are familiar with the ways and beliefs and faiths of primitive races will agree that it is difficult to discover anywhere in the world a race that has not some story of the Deluge, which they have chronicled and localized to fit the understanding and the conditions of the nation that composes their own immediate world.

Amongst the red nations of America I doubt if any two tribes have the same ideas regarding the Flood. Some of the traditions are grotesque in the extreme; some are impressive; some even profound. But of all the stories of the Deluge that I have been able to collect, I know of not a single one that can even begin to equal in beauty of conception, let alone rival in possible reality and truth, the Squamish legend of The Deep Waters.

❦ 229

When a Coast Indian consents to tell you a legend he will, without variation, begin it with: "It was before the white people came."

The natural thing to ask then is: "But who were here then?"

He will reply: "Indians, and just the trees, and animals, and fishes and a few birds."

So you are expected to accept the animal world as intelligent co-habitants of the Pacific slope, but he will not lead you to think he regards them as equals, much less superiors. This is in contrast with "mine own people," the Iroquois tribes of Ontario. They hold the intelligence of wild animals far above that of man, for perhaps the one reason that when an animal is sick, it effects its own cure. It knows what grasses and herbs to eat and what to avoid, while the sick human calls the medicine-man, whose wisdom has been gained only as the result of years of study, handed down from generation to generation. I do not find a single tradition of the Iroquois wherein animals do not play a more important part than humans, and displaying a finer intelligence, and our story of the Deluge rests entirely on the intelligence of sea-going and river-going creatures.

Iroquois tradition tells us that once this earth was entirely submerged in water, and during this period for many days a busy little musk-rat swam about vainly looking for a foothold of earth wherein to build his house. In his search he encountered a turtle, leisurely swimming, and they had speech together. The musk-rat complained of weariness. He could find no foothold, he was tired of incessant swimming, and he longed for land such as his ancestors had enjoyed. The turtle suggested that the musk-rat should dive and try to find earth at the bottom of the sea. Acting on this advice, the musk-rat plunged down, then arose with his two little forepaws grasping some earth he had found beneath the waters.

"Place it on my shell and dive again for more," directed the turtle.

The musk-rat did so, but when he returned with his paws filled with earth he discovered the small quantity he had first deposited on the turtle's shell had doubled in size. The return from the third trip found the turtle's load again doubled. So the building went on at double compound increase, and the world grew its continents and its islands again, all resting on the shell of a turtle.

If you ask the Iroquois story-teller, "And did no men survive this flood?" he will reply: "Why should men survive? The animals are wiser than men; let the wisest live."

How, then, was the earth re-peopled?

The Iroquois will tell you that among the animals was an otter that was a medicine-man. In swimming and diving about, he found corpses of men and women. He sang his medicine songs and they came to life again, and the otter brought them fish for food until they were strong enough to provide for themselves. Then the Iroquois will conclude his tale with: "You know well that the otter has greater wisdom than a man."

Far different is the tradition of the Squamish tribe. It was on a February day that I first listened to this beautiful, homane, story of the Deluge. My royal old friend had come to see me through the rains and mists of late winter. The gateways of my wigwam always stood open — very widely open — for his feet to enter, and this especial day he came with the worst downpour of the season.

Woman-like, I protested with a thousand contradictions in my voice, that he should venture out to see me on such a day. It was, "Oh, Chief, I am so glad to see you." And it was, "Oh, Chief, why didn't you stay at home on such a wet day

— your poor throat will suffer." But I soon had quantities of hot tea for him, and the huge cup my own father always used was his — for as long as the Sagalie Tyee allowed his dear feet to wander my way. The immense cup stands idle and empty now for the second time.

Helping him off with his great-coat, I chatted on about the deluge of rain, and he remarked it was not so very bad, as one could yet walk.

"Fortunately, yes, for I cannot swim," I told him.

He laughed, replying: "Well, it is not as bad as when the great deep waters covered the world."

Immediately I foresaw the coming of a legend. "No?" I encouraged him.

"No," he replied. "For, one time, there was no land here at all; everywhere there was just water."

"I can quite believe it," I remarked caustically.

He laughed, that irresistible, though silent, laugh of his that always brought a responsive smile from his listeners. Then he plunged directly into the tradition, with no preface save a comprehensive sweep of his hands towards my wide windows against which the rains were beating.

"It was after a long, long time of this — this rain. The mountain-streams were swollen, the rivers choked, the sea began to rise, and yet it rained; for weeks and weeks it rained." He ceased speaking while the shadows of centuries gone crept into his eyes. Tales of the misty past always inspired him.

"Yes," he contined. "It rained for weeks and weeks, while the mountain torrents roared thunderingly down and the sea crept silently up. The level lands were first to float in sea-water, then to disappear. The slopes were next to slip under the sea. The world was slowly being flooded. Hurriedly the Indian tribes gathered in one spot, a place of safety far above the reach of the on-creeping sea. The spot was the circling shore of Lake Beautiful, up the North Arm. They held a Great Council and decided at once upon a plan of action. A giant canoe should be built, and some means contrived to anchor it in case the waters mounted to the heights. The men undertook the canoe, the women the anchorage.

"A giant tree was felled, and day and night the men toiled over its construction into the most stupendous canoe the world has even known. Not an hour, not a moment, but many worked, while the toil-wearied ones slept, only to wake to renewed toil. Meanwhile, the women also worked at a cable — the largest, the longest, the strongest that Indian hands and teeth had ever made. Scores of them gathered and prepared the cedar-fibre; scores of them plaited, rolled and seasoned it; scores of them chewed upon it inch by inch to make it pliable; scores of them oiled and worked it into a sea-resisting fabric. And still the sea crept up, and up, and up. It was the last day. Hope of life for the tribes, of land for the world, was doomed. Strong hands, self-sacrificing hands, fastened the cable the women had made, one end to the giant canoe, the other about an enormous boulder, a vast immovable rock as firm as the foundations of the world — for might not the canoe with its priceless freight, drift out, far out, to sea, and when the water subsided might not this ship of safety be leagues and leagues beyond the sight of land on the storm-driven Pacific?

"Then, with the bravest hearts that ever beat, noble hands lifted every child of the tribes into this vast canoe. Not one single baby was overlooked. The canoe was stocked with food and fresh water, and, lastly, the ancient men and women of the race selected as guardians to these children the bravest, most stalwart, handsomest young man of the tribes, and the mother of the youngest baby in the camp — a brave and very beautiful girl of sixteen, her child but two weeks old. These two were placed, she at the bow of the

❧ 233

canoe to watch, he at the stern to guide, and all the little children crowded between.

"And still the sea crept up, and up, and up. At the crest of the bluffs about Lake Beautiful the doomed tribes crowded. Not a single person attempted to enter the canoe. There was no wailing, no crying out for safety. Let the little children, the young mother, and the bravest and best of our young men live, was all the farewell those in the canoe heard as the waters reached the summit, and the canoe floated. Last of all to be seen was the top of the tallest tree, then all was a world of water.

"For days and days there was no land, just the swirling, snarling sea, but the canoe rode safely at anchor. The cable those scores of dead, faithful women had made held true as the hearts that beat behind the toil and labour of it all.

"But one morning, at sunrise, far to the South, a speck floated on the breast of the waters. By midday it was larger. At evening it was yet larger. The moon arose and in its magic light the man at the stern saw it was a patch of land. All night he watched it grow, and at day-break looked with glad eyes upon the summit of Mount Baker. He cut the cable, grasped his paddle in his strong hands, and steered for the south. When they landed, the waters were shrunken half down the mountain-side. The children were lifted out. The beautiful young mother, the stalwart young brave, turned to each other, clasped hands, looked into each other's eyes, and smiled.

"And down in the vast country that lies between Mount Baker and the Fraser River they made a new camp, built new lodges, where the little children grew and thrived, and lived and loved, and the earth was repeopled by them.

"The Squamish say that in a gigantic crevice half-way to the crest of Mount Baker may yet be seen the outlines of an enormous canoe, but I have never seen it myself."

❦ 234

He ceased speaking with that far-off cadence in his voice with which he always ended a legend, and for a long time we both sat in silence listening to the rain that was still beating against the windows.

*First published Dominion Illustrated
February, 1893*

"Be pretty good to her, Charlie, my
boy, or she'll balk sure as shooting."

That was what old Jimmy Robinson said to his brand
new son-in-law, while they waited for the bride to reappear.

"Oh! you bet, there's no danger of much else. I'll be good
to her, help me Heaven," replied Charlie McDonald, brightly.

"Yes, of course you will," answered the old man, "but
don't you forget, there's a good big bit of her mother in her,
and," closing his left eye significantly, "you don't understand these Indians as I do."

"But I'm just as fond of them, Mr Robinson," Charlie said
assertively, "and I get on with them too, now, don't I?"

"Yes, pretty well for a town boy; but when you have lived
forty years among these people, as I have done; when you
have had your wife as long as I have had mine — for there's
no getting over it, Christine's disposition is as native as her
mother's, every bit — and perhaps when you've owned for
eighteen years a daughter as dutiful, as loving, as fearless,
and, alas! as obstinate as that little piece you are stealing
away from me to-day — I tell you, youngster, you'll know

more than you know now. It is kindness for kindness, bullet for bullet, blood for blood. Remember, what you are, she will be," and the old Hudson Bay trader scrutinized Charlie McDonald's face like a detective.

It was a happy, fair face, good to look at, with a certain ripple of dimples somewhere about the mouth, and eyes that laughed out the very sunniness of their owner's soul. There was not a severe nor yet a weak line anywhere. He was a well-meaning young fellow, happily dispositioned, and a great favorite with the tribe at Robinson's Post, whither he had gone in the service of the Department of Agriculture, to assist the local agent through the tedium of a long census-taking.

As a boy he had had the Indian relic-hunting craze, as a youth he had studied Indian archaeology and folk-lore, as a man he consummated his predilections for Indianology by loving, winning and marrying the quiet little daughter of the English trader, who himself had married a native woman some twenty years ago. The country was all backwoods, and the Post miles and miles from even the semblance of civilization, and the lonely young Englishman's heart had gone out to the girl who, apart from speaking a very few words of English, was utterly uncivilized and uncultured, but had withal that marvellously innate refinement so universally possessed by the higher tribes of North American Indians.

Like all her race, observant, intuitive, having a horror of ridicule, consequently quick at acquirement and teachable in mental and social habits, she had developed from absolute pagan indifference into a sweet, elderly Christian woman, whose broken English, quiet manner, and still handsome copper-colored face, were the joy of old Robinson's declining years.

He had given their daughter Christine all the advantages of his own learning — which, if truthfully told, was not universal; but the girl had a fair common education, and the native adaptability to progress.

She belonged to neither and still to both types of the cultured Indian. The solemn, silent, almost heavy manner of the one so commingled with the gesticulating Frenchiness and vivacity of the other, that one unfamiliar with native Canadian life would find it difficult to determine her nationality.

She looked very pretty to Charles McDonald's loving eyes, as she reappeared in the doorway, holding her mother's hand and saying some happy words of farewell. Personally she looked much the same as her sisters, all Canada through, who are the offspring of red and white parentage — olive-complexioned, grey-eyed, black-haired, with figure slight and delicate, and the wistful, unfathomable expression in her whole face that turns one so heart-sick as they glance at the young Indians of to-day — it is the forerunner too frequently of "the white man's disease," consumption — but McDonald was pathetically in love, and thought her the most beautiful woman he had ever seen in his life.

There had not been much of a wedding ceremony. The priest had cantered through the service in Latin, pronounced the benediction in English, and congratulated the "happy couple" in Indian, as a compliment to the assembled tribe in the little amateur structure that did service at the post as a sanctuary.

But the knot was tied as firmly and indissolubly as if all Charlie McDonald's swell city friends had crushed themselves up against the chancel to congratulate him, and in his heart he was deeply thankful to escape the flower-pelting, white gloves, rice-throwing, and ponderous stupidity of a breakfast, and indeed all the regulation gimcracks of the usual marriage celebrations, and it was with a hand trembling with absolute happiness that he assisted his little Indian wife into the old muddy buckboard that, hitched to an underbred-looking pony, was to convey them over the first stages of their journey. Then came more adieus, some hand-clasping, old Jimmy Robinson looking very serious just at the last, Mrs. Jimmy, stout, stolid, betraying nothing of visible emotion, and then the pony, rough-shod and shaggy, trudged on, while mutual hand-waves were kept up until the old Hudson's Bay Post dropped out of sight, and the buck-board with its lightsome load of hearts, deliriously happy, jogged on over the uneven trail.

❦

She was "all the rage" that winter at the provincial capi-tal. The men called her a "deuced fine little woman." The ladies said she was "just the sweetest wildflower." Whereas she was really but an ordinary, pale, dark girl who spoke slowly and with a strong accent, who danced fairly well, sang acceptably, and never stirred outside the door without her husband.

Charlie was proud of her; he was proud that she had "taken" so well among his friends, proud that she bore her-self so complacently in the drawing-rooms of the wives of pompous Government officials, but doubly proud of her almost abject devotion to him. If ever human being was wor-shipped that being was Charlie McDonald; it could scarcely have been otherwise, for the almost godlike strength of his passion for that little wife of his would have mastered and melted a far more invincible citadel than an already affec-tionate woman's heart.

Favorites socially, McDonald and his wife went every-where. In fashionable circles she was "new" — a potent charm to acquire popularity, and the little velvet-clad figure was always the centre of interest among all the women in the room. She always dressed in velvet. No woman in Canada, has she but the faintest dash of native blood in her veins, but loves velvets and silks. As beef to the Englishman, wine to the Frenchman, fads to the Yankee, so are velvet and silk to the Indian girl, be she wild as prairie grass, be she on the borders of civilization, or, having stepped within its boundary, mounted the steps of culture even under its superficial heights.

"Such a dolling little appil blossom," said the wife of a local MP, who brushed up her etiquette and English once a year at Ottawa. "Does she always laugh so sweetly, and gobble you up with those great big grey eyes of hers, when you are togetheah at home, Mr. McDonald? If so, I should think youah pooah brothah would feel himself terribly *de trop*."

He laughed lightly. "Yes, Mrs. Stuart, there are not two of Christie; she is the same at home and abroad, and as for Joe, he doesn't mind us a bit; he's no end fond of her."

"I'm very glad he is. I always fancied he did not care for her, d'you know."

If ever a blunt woman existed it was Mrs. Stuart. She really meant nothing, but her remark bothered Charlie. He was fond of his brother, and jealous for Christie's popularity. So that night when he and Joe were having a pipe he said:

"I've never asked you yet what you thought of her, Joe." A brief pause, then Joe spoke. "I'm glad she loves you."

"Why?"

"Because that girl has but two possibilities regarding humanity — love or hate."

"Humph! Does she love or hate *you*?"

"Ask her."

"You talk bosh. If she hated you, you'd get out. If she loved you I'd *make* you get out."

Joe McDonald whistled a little, then laughed.

"Now that we are on the subject, I might as well ask —

honestly, old man, wouldn't you and Christie prefer keeping house alone to having me always around?"

"Nonsense, sheer nonsense. Why, thunder, man, Christie's no end fond of you, and as for me — you surely don't want assurances from me?"

"No, but I often think a young couple —"

"Young couple be blowed! After a while when they want you and your old surveying chains, and spindle-legged tripod telescope kickshaws, farther west, I venture to say the little woman will cry her eyes out — won't you, Christie?" This last in a higher tone, as through clouds of tobacco smoke he caught sight of his wife passing the doorway.

She entered. "Oh, no, I would not cry; I never do cry, but I would be heart-sore to lose you, Joe, and apart from that" — a little wickedly — "you may come in handy for an exchange some day, as Charlie does always say when he hoards up duplicate relics."

"Are Charlie and I duplicates?"

"Well — not exactly" — her head a little to one side, and eyeing them both merrily, while she slipped softly on to the arm of her husband's chair — "but, in the event of Charlie's failing me" — everyone laughed then. The "some day" that she spoke of was nearer than they thought. It came about in this wise.

There was a dance at the Lieutenant-Governor's, and the world and his wife were there. The nobs were in great feather that night, particularly the women, who flaunted about in new gowns and much splendor. Christie McDonald had a new gown also, but wore it with the utmost unconcern, and if she heard any of the flattering remarks made about her she at least appeared to disregard them.

"I never dreamed you could wear blue so splendidly," said Captain Logan, as they sat out a dance together.

"Indeed she can, though," interposed Mrs. Stuart, halting

❦ 242

in one of her gracious sweeps down the room with her husband's private secretary.

"Don't shout so, captain. I can hear every sentence you uttah — of course Mrs. McDonald can wear blue — she has a morning gown of cadet blue that she is a picture in."

"You are both very kind," said Christie. "I like blue; it is the color of all the Hudson's Bay posts, and the factor's residence is always decorated in blue."

"Is it really? How interesting — do tell us some more of your old home, Mrs. McDonald; you so seldom speak of your life at the post, and we fellows so often wish to hear of it all," said Logan eagerly.

"Why do you not ask me of it, then?"

"Well — er, I'm sure I don't know; I'm fully interested in the Ind — in your people — your mother's people, I mean, but it always seems so personal, I suppose; and — a — a — "

"Perhaps you are, like all other white people, afraid to mention my nationality to me."

The captain winced, and Mrs. Stuart laughed uneasily. Joe McDonald was not far off, and he was listening, and chuckling, and saying to himself; "That's you, Christie, lay 'em out; it won't hurt 'em to know how they appear once in a while."

"Well, Captain Logan," she was saying, "what is it you would like to hear — of my people, or my parents, or myself?"

"All, all, my dear," cried Mrs. Stuart clamorously. "I'll speak for him — tell us of yourself and your mother — your father is delightful, I am sure — but then he is only an ordinary Englishman, not half as interesting as a foreigner, or — or, perhaps I should say, a native."

Christie laughed. "Yes," she said, "my father often teases my mother now about how *very* native she was when he married her; then, how could she have been otherwise? She did not know a word of English, and there was not another English-speaking person besides my father and his two companions within sixty miles."

"Two companions, eh? one a Catholic priest and the other a wine merchant, I suppose, and with your father in the Hudson's Bay, they were good representatives of the pioneers in the New World," remarked Logan, waggishly.

"Oh, no, they were all Hudson's Bay men. There were no rumsellers and no missionaries in that part of the country then."

Mrs. Stuart looked puzzled. *"No missionaries?"* she repeated with an odd intonation.

Christie's insight was quick. There was a peculiar expression of interrogation in the eyes of her listeners, and the girl's blood leapt angrily up into her temples as she said hurriedly, "I know what you mean; I know what you are thinking. You are wondering how my parents were married — "

"Well — er, my dear, it seems peculiar — if there was no priest, and no magistrate, why — a — " Mrs. Stuart paused awkwardly.

"The marriage was performed by Indian rites," said Christie.

"Oh, do tell me about it; is the ceremony very interesting and quaint — are your chieftains anything like Buddhist priests?" It was Logan who spoke.

"Why, no," said the girl in amazement at that gentleman's ignorance. "There is no ceremony at all, save a feast. The two people just agree to live only with and for each other, and the man takes his wife to his home, just as you do. There is no ritual to bind them; they need none; an Indian's word was his law in those days, you know."

Mrs. Stuart stepped backwards. "Ah!" was all she said. Logan removed his eye-glass and stared blankly at Christie.

❧ 244

"And did McDonald marry you in this singular fashion?" he questioned.

"Oh, no, we were married by Father O'Leary. Why do you ask?"

"Because if he had, I'd have blown his brains out to-morrow."

Mrs. Stuart's partner, who had hitherto been silent, coughed and began to twirl his cuff stud nervously, but nobody took any notice of him. Christie had risen, slowly, ominously — risen, with the dignity and pride of an empress.

"Captain Logan," she said, "what do you dare to say to me? What do you dare to mean? Do you presume to think it would not have been lawful for Charlie to marry me according to my people's rites? Do you for one instant dare to question that my parents were not as legally — "

"Don't, dear, don't," interrupted Mrs. Stuart hurriedly; "it is bad enough now, goodness knows; don't make — " Then she broke off blindly. Christie's eyes glared at the mumbling woman, at her uneasy partner, at the horrified captain. Then they rested on the McDonald brothers, who stood within earshot, Joe's face scarlet, her husband's white as ashes, with something in his eyes she had never seen before. It was Joe who saved the situation. Stepping quickly across towards his sister-in-law, he offered her his arm, saying, "The next dance is ours, I think, Christie."

Then Logan pulled himself together, and attempted to carry Mrs. Stuart off for the waltz, but for once in her life that lady had lost her head. "It is shocking!" she said, "outrageously shocking! I wonder if they told Mr. McDonald before he married her!" Then looking hurriedly round, she too saw the young husband's face — and knew that they had not.

"Humph! deuced nice kettle of fish — poor old Charlie has always thought so much of honorable birth."

❦ 245

Logan thought he spoke in an undertone, but "poor old Charlie" heard him. He followed his wife and brother across the room. "Joe," he said, "will you see that a trap is called?" Then to Christie, "Joe will see that you get home all right." He wheeled on his heel then and left the ball-room.

Joe *did* see.

He tucked a poor, shivering, pallid little woman into a cab, and wound her bare throat up in the scarlet velvet cloak that was hanging uselessly over her arm. She crouched down beside him, saying, "I am so cold, Joe; I am so cold," but she did not seem to know enough to wrap herself up. Joe felt all through this long drive that nothing this side of Heaven would be so good as to die, and he was glad when the poor little voice at his elbow said, "What is he so angry at, Joe?"

"I don't know exactly, dear," he said gently, "but I think it was what you said about this Indian marriage."

"But why should I not have said it? Is there anything wrong about it?" she asked pitifully.

"Nothing, that I can see — there was no other way; but Charlie is very angry, and you must be brave and forgiving with him, Christie, dear."

"But I did never see him like that before, did you?"

"Once."

"When?"

"Oh, at college, one day, a boy tore his prayer book in half, and threw it into the grate, just to be mean, you know. Our mother had given it to him at his confirmation."

"And did he look so?"

"About, but it all blew over in a day — Charlie's tempers are short and brisk. Just don't take any notice of him; run off to bed, and he'll have forgotten it by the morning."

They reached home at last. Christie said good-night quietly, going directly to her room. Joe went to his room also, filled a pipe and smoked for an hour. Across the passage he could hear her slippered feet pacing up and down, up and down the length of her apartment. There was something panther-like in those restless footfalls, a meaning velvetyness that made him shiver, and again he wished he were dead — or elsewhere.

After a time the hall door opened, and someone came upstairs, along the passage, and to the little woman's room. As he entered, she turned and faced him.

"Christie," he said harshly, "do you know what you have done?"

"Yes," taking a step nearer him, her whole soul springing up into her eyes," I have angered you, Charlie, and — "

"Angered me? You have disgraced me; and, moreover, you have disgraced yourself and both your parents."

"*Disgraced?*"

"Yes, *disgraced*; you have literally declared to the whole city that your father and mother were never married, and that you are the child of — what shall we call it — love? certainly not legality."

Across the hallway sat Joe McDonald, his blood freezing; but it leapt into every vein like fire at the awful anguish in the little voice that cried simply, "Oh! Charlie!"

"How could you do it, how could you do it, Christie, without shame either for yourself or for me, let alone your parents?"

The voice was like an angry demon's — not a trace was there in it of the yellow-haired, blue-eyed, laughing-lipped boy who had driven away so gaily to the dance five hours before.

"Shame? Why should I be ashamed of the rites of my people any more than you should be ashamed of the customs of yours — of a marriage more sacred and holy than half of your white man's mockeries?"

❦ 247

It was the voice of another nature in the girl — the love and the pleading were dead in it.

"Do you mean to tell me, Charlie — you who have studied my race and their laws for years — do you mean to tell me that, because there was no priest and no magistrate, my mother was not married? Do you mean to say that all my forefathers, for hundreds of years back, have been illegally born? If so, you blacken my ancestry beyond — beyond — beyond all reason."

"No, Christie, I would not be so brutal as that; but your father and mother live in more civilized times. Father O'Leary has been at the post for nearly twenty years. Why was not your father straight enough to have the ceremony performed when he *did* get the chance?"

The girl turned upon him with the face of a fury. "Do you suppose," she almost hissed, "that my mother would be married according to your *white* rites after she had been five years a wife, and I had been born in the meantime? *No*, a thousand times I say, *no*. When the priest came with his notions of Christianizing, and talked to them of re-marriage by the Church, my mother arose and said, "Never — never — I have never had but this one husband; he has had none but me for wife, and to have you re-marry us would be to say as much to the whole world as that we had never been married before. You go away; *I* do not ask that *your* people be re-married; talk not so to me. I *am* married, and you or the Church cannot do or undo it."

"Your father was a fool not to insist upon the law, and so was the priest."

"Law? *My* people have *no* priest, and my nation cringes not to law. Our priest is purity, and our law is honor. Priest? Was there a *priest* at the most holy marriage known to humanity — that stainless marriage whose offspring is the God you white men told my pagan mother of?"

"Christie — you are *worse* than blasphemous; such a profane remark shows how little you understand the sanctity of the Christian faith — "

"I know what I *do* understand; it is that you are hating me because I told some of the beautiful customs of my people to Mrs. Stuart and those men."

"Pooh! who cares for them? It is not them; the trouble is they won't keep their mouths shut. Logan's a cad and will toss the whole tale about at the club before to-morrow night; and as for the Stuart woman, I'd like to know how I'm going to take you to Ottawa for presentation and the opening, while she is babbling the whole miserable scandal in every drawing-room, and I'll be pointed out as a romantic fool, and you — as worse; I *can't* understand why your father didn't tell me before we were married; I at least might have warned you to never mention it." Something of recklessness rang up through his voice, just as the panther-likeness crept up from her footsteps and couched itself in hers. She spoke in tones quiet, soft, deadly.

"Before we were married! Oh! Charlie, would it have — made — any — difference?"

"God knows," he said, throwing himself into a chair, his blonde hair rumpled and wet. It was the only boyish thing about him now.

She walked towards him, then halted in the centre of the room. "Charlie McDonald," she said, and it was as if a stone had spoken, "look up." He raised his head, startled by her tone. There was a threat in her eyes that, had his rage been less courageous, his pride less bitterly wounded, would have cowed him.

"There was no such time as that before our marriage, for we *are not married now*. Stop," she said, outstretching her palms against him as he sprang to his feet, "I tell you we are not married. Why should I recognize the rites of your nation

❦ 249

when you do not acknowledge the rites of mine? According to your own words, my parents should have gone through your church ceremony as well as through an Indian contract; according to *my* words, *we* should go through an Indian contract as well as through a church marriage. If their union is illegal, so is ours. If you think my father is living in dishonor with my mother, my people will think I am living in dishonor with you. How do I know when another nation will come and conquer you as you white men conquered us? And they will have another marriage rite to perform, and they will tell us another truth, that you are not my husband, that you are but disgracing and dishonoring me, that you are keeping me here, not as your wife, but as your — your *squaw*."

The terrible word had never passed her lips before, and the blood stained her face to her very temples. She snatched off her wedding ring and tossed it across the room, saying scornfully, "That thing is as empty to me as the Indian rites to you."

He caught her by the wrists; his small white teeth were locked tightly, his blue eyes blazed into hers.

"Christine, do you dare to doubt my honor towards you? *you*, whom I should have died for; do you *dare* to think I have kept you here, not as my wife, but — "

"Oh, God! You are hurting me; you are breaking my arm," she gasped.

The door was flung open, and Joe McDonald's sinewy hands clinched like vices on his brother's shoulders.

"Charlie, you're mad, mad as the devil. Let go of her this minute."

The girl staggered backwards as the iron fingers loosed her wrists. "Oh, Joe," she cried, "I am not his wife, and he says I am born — nameless."

"Here," said Joe, shoving his brother towards the door.

"Go downstairs till you can collect your senses. If ever a being acted like an infernal fool, you're the man."

The young husband looked from one to the other, dazed by his wife's insult, abandoned to a fit of ridiculously childish temper. Blind as he was with passion, he remembered long afterwards seeing them standing there, his brother's face darkened with a scowl of anger — his wife, clad in the mockery of her ball dress, her scarlet velvet cloak half covering her bare brown neck and arms, her eyes like flames of fire, her face like a piece of sculptured greystone.

Without a word he flung himself furiously from the room, and immediately afterwards they heard the heavy hall door bang behind him.

"Can I do anything for you, Christie?" asked her brother-in-law calmly.

"No, thank you — unless — I think I would like a drink of water, please."

He brought her up a goblet filled with wine; her hand did not even tremble as she took it. As for Joe, a demon arose in his soul as he noticed she kept her wrists covered.

"Do you think he will come back?" she said.

"Oh, yes, of course; he'll be all right in the morning. Now go to bed like a good little girl, and — and, I say, Christie, you can call me if you want anything; I'll be right here, you know."

"Thank you, Joe; you are kind — and good."

He returned then to his apartment. His pipe was out, but he picked up a newspaper instead, threw himself into an armchair, and in a half-hour was in the land of dreams.

When Charlie came home in the morning, after a six-mile walk into the country and back again, his foolish anger was dead and buried. Logan's "Poor old Charlie" did not ring so distinctly in his ears. Mrs. Stuart's horrified expression had faded considerably from his recollection. He thought only of that surprisingly tall, dark girl, whose eyes looked like coals, whose voice pierced him like a flint-tipped arrow. Ah, well, they would never quarrel again like that, he told himself. She loved him so, and would forgive him after he had talked quietly to her, and told her what an ass he was. She was simple-minded and awfully ignorant to pitch those old Indian laws at him in her fury, but he could not blame her; oh, no, he could not for one moment blame her. He had been terribly severe and unreasonable, and the horrid McDonald temper had got the better of him; and he loved her so. Oh! he loved her so! She would surely feel that, and forgive him, and — He went straight to his wife's room. The blue velvet evening dress lay on the chair into which he had thrown himself when he doomed his life's happiness by those two words, "God knows." A bunch of dead daffodils and her slippers were on the floor, everything — but Christie.

He went to his brother's bedroom door.

"Joe," he called, rapping nervously thereon; "Joe, wake up; where's Christie, d'you know?"

"Good Lord, no," gasped that youth, springing out of his armchair and opening the door. As he did so a note fell from off the handle. Charlie's face blanched to his very hair while Joe read aloud, his voice weakening at every word:

"DEAR OLD JOE — *I went into your room at daylight to get that picture of the Post on your bookshelves. I hope you do not mind, but I kissed your hair while you slept; it was so curly, and yellow, and soft, just like his. Good-bye, Joe.*
                                                                    "CHRISTIE."

And when Joe looked into his brother's face and saw the anguish settle in those laughing blue eyes, the despair that drove the dimples away from that almost girlish mouth; when he realized that this boy was but four-and-twenty years old, and that all his future was perhaps darkened and shadowed for ever, a great, deep sorrow arose in his heart, and he forgot all things, all but the agony that rang up through the voice of the fair, handsome lad as he staggered forward, crying, "Oh! Joe — what shall I do — what shall I do?"

It was months and months before he found her, but during all that time he had never known a hopeless moment; discouraged he often was, but despondent, never. The sunniness of his ever-boyish heart radiated with a warmth that would have flooded a much deeper gloom than that which settled within his eager young life. Suffer? ah! yes, he suffered, not with locked teeth and stony stoicism, not with the masterful self-command, the reserve, the conquered bitterness of the still-water sort of nature, that is supposed to run to such depths. He tried to be bright, and his sweet old boyish self. He would laugh sometimes in a pitiful, pathetic fashion. He took to petting dogs, looking into their large, solemn eyes with his wistful, questioning blue ones; he would kiss them, as women sometimes do, and call them "dear old fellow," in tones that had tears; and once in the course of his travels, while at a little way-station, he discovered a huge St. Bernard imprisoned by some mischance in an empty freight car; the animal was nearly dead from starvation, and it seemed to salve his own sick heart to rescue back the dog's life. Nobody claimed the big starving creature, the train hands knew nothing of its owner, and gladly handed it over to its deliverer. "Hudson," he called it, and afterwards when Joe McDonald would relate the story of his brother's life he invariably terminated it with, "And I really believe that big lumbering brute saved him." From what, he was never known to say.

But all things end, and he heard of her at last. She had never returned to the Post, as he at first thought she would, but had gone to the little town of B——, in Ontario, where she was making her living at embroidery and plain sewing.

The September sun had set redly when at last he reached the outskirts of the town, opened up the wicket gate, and walked up the weedy, unkept path leading to the cottage where she lodged.

Even through the twilight, he could see her there, leaning on the rail of the verandah — oddly enough she had about her shoulders the scarlet velvet cloak she wore when he had flung himself so madly from the room that night.

The moment the lad saw her his heart swelled with a sudden heat, burning moisture leapt into his eyes, and clogged his long, boyish lashes. He bounded up the steps — "Christie," he said, and the word scorched his lips like audible flame.

She turned to him, and for a second stood magnetized by his passionately wistful face; her peculiar greyish eyes seemed to drink the very life of his unquenchable love, though the tears that suddenly sprang into his seemed to absorb every pulse in his body through those hungry, pleading eyes of his that had, oh! so often, been blinded by her kisses when once her whole world lay in their blue depths.

"You will come back to me, Christie, my wife? My wife, you will let me love you again?"

She gave a singular little gasp, and shook her head. "Don't, oh! don't," he cried piteously. "You will come to me, dear? it is all such a bitter mistake — I did not understand. Oh! Christie, I did not understand, and you'll forgive me, and love me again, won't you — won't you?"

"No," said the girl with quick, indrawn breath.

He dashed the back of his hand across his wet eyelids. His lips were growing numb, and he bungled over the monosyllable "Why?"

"I do not like you," she answered quietly.

"God! Oh! God, what is there left?"

She did not appear to hear the heart break in his voice; she stood like one wrapped in sombre thought; no blaze, no tear, nothing in her eyes; no hardness, no tenderness about her mouth. The wind was blowing her cloak aside, and the only visible human life in her whole body was once when he spoke the muscles of her brown arm seemed to contract.

"But, darling, you are mine — *mine* — we are husband and wife! Oh, heaven, you *must* love me, you *must* come to me again."

"You cannot *make* me come," said the icy voice, "neither church, nor law, nor even" — and the voice softened — "nor even love can make a slave of a red girl."

"Heaven forbid it," he faltered. "No, Christie, I will never claim you without your love. What reunion would that be? But, oh, Christie, you are lying to me, you are lying to yourself, you are lying to heaven."

She did not move. If only he could touch her he felt as sure of her yielding as he felt sure there was a hereafter. The memory of times when he had but to lay his hand on her hair to call a most passionate response from her filled his heart with a torture that chocked all words before they reached his lips; at the thought of those days he forgot she was unapproachable, forgot how forbidding were her eyes, how stony her lips. Flinging himself forward, his knee on the chair at her side, his face pressed hardly in the folds of the cloak on her shoulder, he clasped his arms about her with a boyish petulance, saying, "Christie, Christie, my little girl wife, I love you, I love you, and you are killing me."

❦ 255

She quivered from head to foot as his fair, wavy hair brushed her neck, his despairing face sank lower until his cheek, hot as fire, rested on the cool, olive flesh of her arm. A warm moisture oozed up through her skin, and as he felt its glow he looked up. Her teeth, white and cold, were locked over her under lip, and her eyes were as grey stones.

Not all murderers alone know the agony of a death sentence.

"Is it all useless? All useless, dear?" he said, with lips starving for hers.

"All useless," she repeated. "I have no love for you now. You forfeited me and my heart months ago, when you said *those two words.*"

His arms fell away from her wearily, he arose mechanically, he placed his little grey checked cap on the back of his yellow curls, the old-time laughter was dead in the blue eyes that now looked scared and haunted, the boyishness and the dimples crept away for ever from the lips that quivered like a child's; he turned from her, but she had looked once into his face as the Law Giver must have looked at the land of Canaan outspread at his feet. She watched him go down the long path and through the picket gate, she watched the big yellowish dog that had waited for him lumber up to its feet — stretch — then follow him. She was conscious of but two things, the vengeful lie in her soul, and a little space on her arm that his wet lashes had brushed.

❧ A NIGHT WITH NORTH EAGLE

*First published Boy's World
January 18, 1908*

The great transcontinental express was swinging through the Canadian northwest into the land of the setting sun. Its powerful engine throbbed along the level track of the prairie. The express, mail, baggage, first-class and sleeping coaches followed like the pliant tail of a huge eel. Then the wheels growled out the tones of lessening speed. The giant animal slowed up, then came to a stand-still. The stop awoke Norton Allan, who rolled over in his berth with a peculiar wide-awake sensation, and waited vainly for the train to resume its flight towards the Rockies. Some men seemed to be trailing up and down outside the Pullman car, so Norton ran up the little window blind and looked out. Just a small station platform of a small prairie settlement was all he saw but he hear voices very distinctly.

"What place is this?" someone asked.

"Gleichen, about sixty miles east of Calgary."

"Construction camp?"

Someone laughed. "No. This line was laid about the time you were born, I guess."

"What are all those tents, over there?"

"Indian tepees. This is the heart of the Blackfoot Reserve."

Norton's heart gave a great throb. The far-famed Black-foot Indians! And just outside his Pullman window. . . .

Oh, if the train would only wait there until morning! As if in answer to his wish, a quick alert voice cut in saying, "Washout ahead, boys. The Bow River's been cutting up. We're stalled here for good and all, I guess." And the lanterns and voices faded away forward.

Norton lay very still for a few moments trying to realize it all. Then raising himself on one elbow, he peered out across an absolutely level open prairie. A waning moon hung low in the west, its thin radiance brooding above the plains like a mist, but the light was sufficient to reveal some half-dozen tepees, that lifted their smoky tops and tent poles not three hundred yards from the railway track. Norton looked at his watch. He could just make out that it was two o'clock in the morning. Could he *ever* wait until daylight? So he asked himself over and over again, while his head (with its big mop of hair that *would* curl in spite of the hours he spent in trying to brush it straight) snuggled down among the pillows, and his grave young eyes blinked longingly at those covered tepees. And the next thing he knew a face was thrust between his berth-curtains, a thin, handsome, clean-shaven face, adorned with gold-rimmed nose glasses, and crowned with a crop of hair much like his own, and a voice he loved very much was announcing in imitation of the steward, "Breakfast is now ready in the dining car."

Norton sprang up, pitching the blankets aside, and seized Professor Allan by the arm. "Oh, Pater," he cried, pointing to the window, "do you see them — the Indians, the tepees? It's the Blackfoot Reserve! I heard the trainmen say so in the night."

"Yes, my boy," replied the Professor, seating himself on the edge of his son's berth. "And I also see your good mother and estimable father dying of starvation, if they have to

❧ 258

wait much longer for you to appear with them in the dining car — "

But Norton was already scrambling into his clothes, his usually solemn eyes shining with excitement. For years his father, who was professor in one of the great universities in Toronto, had shared his studies on Indian life, character, history and habits with his only son. They had read together, and together had collected a splendid little museum of Indian relics and curios. They had always admired the fine old warlike Blackfoot nation, but never did they imagine when they set forth on this summer vacation trip to the Coast, that they would find themselves stalled among these people of their dreams.

"Well, Tony, boy, this *is* a treat for you and father," his mother's voice was saying, "and the conductor tells me we shall be here probably forty-eight hours. The Bow River is on the rampage, the bridge near Calgary is washed away, and thank goodness we shall be comfortably housed and fed in this train." And Mrs. Allan's smiling face appeared beside the Professor's.

"Tony," as his parents called him, had never dressed so quickly in all the sixteen years of his life, notwithstanding the cramped space of a sleeping car, and presently he was seated in the diner, where the broad windows disclosed a sweeping view of the scattered tepees, each with its feather of upward floating smoke curling away from its apex. Many of the Indians were already crowding about the train, some with polished buffalo horns for sale, and all magnificently dressed in buckskin, decorated with fine, old-fashioned bead work, and the quills of the porcupine.

An imperial-looking figure stood somewhat back from the others, exceptionally tall, with finely cut profile, erect shoulders, rich copper-colored skin, and long black hair interbraided with ermine tails and crested with a perfect black and white eagle plume; over his costly buckskins he wore a brilliant green blanket, and he stood with arms folded across his chest with the air of one accustomed to command. Beside him stood a tall, slender boy, his complete counterpart in features and dress, save that boy's blanket was scarlet, and he wore no eagle plume.

"What magnificent manhood!" remarked the Professor. "No college our civilization can boast of will ever give what plain food, simple hours, and the glorious freedom of this prairie air have given that brave and his boy. We must try to speak with them, Tony. I wonder how we can introduce ourselves."

"Some circumstances will lead to it, you may be sure," said Mrs. Allan, cheerfully. "You and Tony walk out for some fresh air. Something will happen, you'll see." And it did.

Crowds of the train's passengers were strolling up and down when the Professor and Norton went outside. "I wish they would not stand and stare at the Indians like that!" remarked the boy indignantly. "The Indians don't stare at us."

"For the best of all reasons," said the Professor. "Indians are taught from the cradle that the worst possible breach of politeness is to stare." And just as they began a little chat on the merits of this teaching, a dapper, well-dressed passenger walked up to the distinguished Indian, and in a very loud voice said, "Good morning, friend. I'd like to buy that eagle feather you have in your hair. Will you sell it? Here's a dollar."

Instantly Norton Allan turned angrily to the passenger. "What do you shout at him for?" he demanded. "He isn't deaf because he's Indian."

"Oh!" said the passenger, rather sheepishly, but in a much lower tone. Then, still raising his voice again, he persisted, "Here's two dollars for your feather."

The Indian never even glanced at him, but with a peculiar, half regal lift of his shoulders, hitched his blanket about him, turned on his heel, and walked slowly away. Just then the train conductor walked past, and the bewildered passenger assailed him with, "I say, conductor, that Indian over there wouldn't take two dollars for that chicken wing in his hair."

The conductor laughed. "I should think not!" he said. " 'That Indian' is Chief Sleeping Thunder, and ten miles across the prairie there, he has three thousand head of cattle, eighty horses, and about two thousand acres of land for them to range over. *He* doesn't want your two dollars."

"Oh!" said the passenger again, this time a little more sheepishly than before; then he wisely betook himself to the train.

Meantime the boy with the scarlet blanket had not moved an inch, only let his eyes rest briefly on Norton when the latter had reproved the shouting passenger.

"And this," continued the conductor kindly, as he paused beside the boy, "is Chief Sleeping Thunder's son, North Eagle."

Norton Allan stepped eagerly forward, raised his cap, and holding out his hand shyly, said, "May I have the pleasure of shaking hands with you, North Eagle?"

The Indian boy extended his own slim brown fingers, a quick smile swept across his face, and he said, "*You* not speak loud." Then they all laughed together, and the Professor, who had been a silent but absorbed onlooker, was soon chatting away with the two boys, as if he too were but sixteen years old, with all the world before him.

That was a memorable day for Norton, for, of course, he met Chief Sleeping Thunder, who, however, could speak but little English; but so well did the friendship progress that at noon North Eagle approached the Professor with the request that Norton should ride with him over to his father's range, sleep in their tepee that night, and return the following morning before the train pulled out.

At North Eagle's shoulder stood Sleeping Thunder, nodding assent to all his son said.

Of course, Mrs. Allan was for politely refusing the invitation. She would not for a moment listen to such an idea. But the Professor took quite the opposite stand. "We must let him go, mother — let him go, by all means. Tony can take care of himself, and it will be the chance of his life. Why, he is nearing manhood now. Let him face the world; let him have this wonderful experience."

"But they look so wild!" pleaded the poor mother. "They *are* wild. Fancy letting our Tony go alone into the heart of the Blackfoot country! Oh! I can't think of it!"

Fortunately for her peace of mind the train conductor overheard her words, and smiling at her fears, said, rather dryly:

"Madam, if your boy is as safe from danger and harm and evil in the city of Toronto as he will be with North Eagle in the prairie country, why, I congratulate you."

The words seemed to sting the good lady. She felt, rather than knew, the truth of them, and the next moment her consent was given.

The face of North Eagle seemed transformed when he got her promise to let Tony go. "I bring him back safe, plenty time for train," was all he said.

Then Sleeping Thunder spoke for the first time — spoke but the one word, "Safe." Then pointing across the prairie, he repeated, "Safe."

"That's enough, my dear," said the Professor firmly. "Tony is as safe as in a church."

"Yes," replied Mrs. Allan, "the chief means that word

'safe.' And as for that boy, I believe he would die before he'd let Tony's little finger be harmed."

And as events proved, she was almost right.

Within the hour they were off, North Eagle bareback on a wiry cayuse, Tony in a Mexican saddle, astride a beautiful little broncho that loped like a rocking-horse.

At the last minute, Sleeping Thunder was detained by cattlemen, who wanted to purchase some of his stock, so the two boys set out alone. The last good-bye was to the conductor, who, after charging them to return in ample time to catch the train, said seriously to Norton:

"Let nothing scare you, sonny. These Indians *look* savage, in their paint and feathers, but King Edward of England has no better subjects; and I guess it is all the same to His Majesty whether a good subject dresses in buckskin or broadcloth."

Then there was much waving of hats and handkerchiefs. The engineer caught the spirit of the occasion, and genially blew a series of frantic toots, and with the smile of his father and the face of his mother as the last things in his vision, and with North Eagle's scarlet blanket rocking at his elbow, young Norton Allan hit the trail for the heart of the Blackfoot country.

For miles they rode in silence. Twice North Eagle pointed ahead, without speech — first at a coyote, then at a small herd of antelope, and again at a band of Indian riders whose fleet ponies and gay trappings crossed the distant horizon like a meteor.

By some marvellous intuition North Eagle seemed to know just what would interest the white boy — all the romance of the trail, the animals, the game, the cactus beds, the vast areas of mushrooms growing wild, edible and luscious, the badger and gopher holes, and the long, winding, half-obliterated buffalo trails that yet scarred the distant reaches. It was only when he pointed to these latter, that he really spoke his mind, breaking into an eloquence that filled Tony with envy. The young redskin seemed inspired; a perfect torrent of words rushed to his lips, then his voice saddened as he concluded: "But they will never come again, the mighty buffalo my father and my grandfather used to chase. They have gone, gone to a far country, for they loved not the ways of the paleface. Sometimes at night I dream I hear their thousand hoofs beat up the trail, I see their tossing horns, like the prairie grass in the strong west winds, but they are only spirits now; they will never come to me, and I have waited so long, so many days, watching these trails, watching, watching, watching — but they never come; no, the buffalo never come."

Tony did not speak. What was there to be said? He only shook his head comprehendingly, and bit his under lip hard to keep back — something, he scarcely knew what. But he too watched the buffalo runs with longing eyes, hoping, hoping that even *one* glorious animal would gallop up out of the rim of grass and sky. But young North Eagle was right — the buffalo was no more.

Tony was just beginning to feel slightly sore in the saddle when the Indian pointed off to the southwest and said, "There is my father's tepee," and within five minutes they had slipped from their mounts, and stood on the Chief's domain. A woman, followed by three children, came to the door. She was very handsome, and wore the beautiful dress of her tribe. Her cheeks were painted a brilliant crimson, and the parting of her hair was stained a rich orange. North Eagle turned and spoke rapidly to her for a moment in the Blackfoot tongue. She replied briefly. "Here is my mother," said the boy simply. "She speaks no English, but she says you are welcome and her heart is warm for you."

Tony lifted his cap while he shook hands. The woman noiselessly put back the door of the tepee and motioned for him to enter. For a moment he thought he must be dreaming. The exterior of the tepee had been wonderful enough, with its painted designs of suns and planets and wolf heads and horses, but the inside betokened such a wealth of Indian possessions that the boy was fairly astounded. The tepee itself was quite thirty feet in diameter, and pitched above dry, brown, clean prairie sod, which, however, was completely concealed by skins of many animals — cinnamon bear, fox, prairie wolf, and badger. To the poles were suspended suit after suit of magnificent buckskin, leggings, shirts, moccasins, all beaded and embroidered in priceless richness, fire bags, tobacco pouches, beaded gun cases, and rabbit robes. Fully a dozen suits were fringed down the sleeves and leggings with numberless ermine tails. At one side of the tepee lay piled quite a score of blankets in mixed colors, a heap of thick furs, pyramids of buffalo horns, and coils and coils of the famous "grass and sinew" lariats for roping cattle and horses.

The contents of that tepee would have brought thousands of dollars in New York City.

Across Norton's mind there flashed the recollection of the passenger offering his paltry two dollars to Sleeping Thunder for the eagle plume in his hair. No wonder the train conductor had laughed! And just here North Eagle entered, asking him if he would care to see the cattle that were ranging somewhere near by. Of course he cared, and for all the years to come he never forgot that sight. For a mile beyond him the landscape seemed blotted out by a sea of gleaming horns and shifting hoofs — a moving mass that seemed to swim into the sky. It was a great possession — a herd like that — and Norton found himself marvelling at the strange fact that he and his parents, travelling in luxurious Pullmans, and living in a great city, were poor in comparison with this slender Blackfoot boy who was acting host with the grace that comes only with perfect freedom and simplicity.

The day was very warm, so supper was prepared outside the tepee, North Eagle showing Tony how to build a fire in a prairie wind, lee of the tepee, and midway between two upright poles supporting a cross-bar from which the kettles hung. Boiled beef, strong black tea, and bannock were the main foods, but out of compliment to their visitor, they fried a quantity of delicious mushrooms, and, although the Black-feet seldom eat them, Tony fairly devoured several helpings. After supper North Eagle took him again into the tepee, and showed him all the wonderful buckskin garments and orna-ments. Tony was speechless with the delight of it all, and even begrudged the hours wherein he must sleep; but the unusual length of the ride, the clear air, and the hearty supper he had eaten, all began to tell on his excitement, and he was quite ready to "turn in" with the others shortly after sunset.

"Turning in" meant undressing, folding a Hudson's Bay blanket about him, and lying near the open flap of the tepee, on a heap of wolf skins as soft as feathers and as silvery as a cloud.

Night crept up over the prairie like a gray veil, and the late moon, rising, touched the far level wastes with a pale radiance. Through the open flap of the tepee Tony watched it — the majestic loneliness and isolation, the hushed silence of this prairie world were very marvellous — and he loved it almost as if it were his birthright, instead of the heritage of the Blackfoot boy sleeping beside him. Then across the white night came the cry of a wandering coyote, and once the whirr of many wings swept overhead. Then his wolf-skin couch grew very soft and warm, the night airs very gentle, the silence very drowsy, and Tony slept.

It was daylight. Something had wakened him abruptly.

❦ 266

Instantly all his faculties were alert, yet oddly enough he seemed held rigid and speechless. He wanted to cry out with fear, he knew not of what, and the next moment a lithe red body was flung across his, and his hand was imprisoned in strong, clinging fingers. There was a brief struggle, a torrent of words he did not understand, a woman's frightened voice. Then the lithe red body, North Eagle's body, lifted itself, and Tony struggled up, white, scared, and bewildered. The Blackfoot boy was crouching at his elbow, and some terrible thing was winding and lashing itself about his thin dark wrist and arm. It seemed a lifetime that Tony's staring eyes were riveted on the horror of the thing, but it really was all over in a moment, and the Indian had choked a brutal rattlesnake, then flung it at his feet. No one spoke for a full minute, then North Eagle said, very quietly, "He curl one foot from your right hand, he lift his head to strike. I wake — I catch him just below his head — he is dead."

Again there was silence. Then North Eagle's mother came slowly, placed one hand on her son's shoulder, the other on Tony's, and looking down at the dead reptile, shook her head meaningly. And Tony, still sitting on the wolf skins, stretched out his arms and clasped them about North Eagle's knees.

Mrs. Allan was right — the Indian boy had risked his life to save her son from danger. Rattlesnakes were so rare in the Blackfoot country that it gave them all a great shock. It was almost too tense and terrible a thing to talk much of, and the strain of it relaxed only when the boys were mounted once more, galloping swiftly away toward Gleichen and the train.

But, notwithstanding this fright, Tony left the tepee with the greatest regret. Before going, North Eagle's mother presented him with a very beautiful pair of moccasins and a valuable string of elk's teeth, and North Eagle translated her good-bye words: "My mother says you will live in her heart; that your hair is very beautiful; that she feels the sun's heat in her heart for you, because you do not speak loud to her."

It was a glorious, breezy gallop of ten miles in the early morning, and as they came up the trail Tony could distinguish his mother, already on the watch, waving a welcome as far as her eyes could discern them. Outside the settlement the boys slackened speed, and talked regretfully of their coming separation. North Eagle was wearing an extremely handsome buckskin shirt, fringed and richly beaded. He began unfastening it. "I give you my shirt," he said. "My mother says it is the best she ever made — it is yours."

For a second Tony's thoughts were busy, then, without hesitation, he too unfastened his shirt, which luckily was a fine blue silk "soft" one. "And I give you mine," he said simply.

Thus did they exchange shirts, and rode up to the station platform, the Indian stripped to the waist with only a scarlet blanket about his shoulders and a roll of blue silk under his arm; the Toronto boy with his coat buttoned up to conceal his underwear, and a gorgeous garment of buckskin across his saddle bow.

The greetings and welcomings were many and merry. Professor and Mrs. Allan were happy and proud in their son, but the shadow of the coming good-bye hung over the boy's face, and he experienced only one glad moment on that platform. It was when Sleeping Thunder came up and, before all the passengers, took the eagle plume from his hair and pressed it into Tony's hand.

"My father says you are brave," explained North Eagle, "and must accept the plume of the brave."

For a moment the clinging fingers of the two boys met, and then Tony found himself fumbling up the steps into the Pullman. And as the train pulled out towards the foothills he stood on the rear platform watching the little station and the tepees slip away, conscious only of two things — that his eyes were seeing it all through a mist that threatened to blind them completely, and that his fingers were holding the eagle plume of Sleeping Thunder.

*An extract from a longer story
first published in The Boy's World,
October, 1908*

If "Fire-flint" Larocque could have
called himself Indian or White he would have known where
he stood, but here he was born to be a thing apart, with no
nationality in all the world to claim as his blood heritage. All
his young life he had been accustomed to hear his parents
and himself referred to as "half-breeds" until one day, when
the Governor-General of all Canada paid a visit to the Indian
school. The principal, with an air of pride, presented "Fire-
Flint" to His Excellency, with "This is our head pupil, the
most diligent boy in the school. He is Trapper Larocque's
son."

"Oh? And what tribe does he belong to?" asked the
Governor as he clasped the boy's hand.

"Fire-Flint belongs to no tribe," explained the principal.
"He's a half-breed."

"Half-breed," repeated the Governor, with a perplexed
wrinkle crossing his brows. "What an odd term. I imagine
you mean a half-blood, not a half-breed."

His voice was chilly and his eyes a little cold as he looked
at the principal. "I do not like the word "breed" applied to
human beings. It is a term for cattle, not men." Then, ad-

dressing Fire-Flint, he asked "Who are your parents, my boy?"

"My father is half French and half Cree; my mother is about three-quarters Cree. Her grandfather was French," explained the boy, while his whole loyal young heart reached out towards this great man who was lifting him out of the depths of obscurity. Then His Excellency's hands rested with a peculiar half-fatherly, half-brotherly touch on the shoulders of the slim lad before him.

"Then you have blood in your veins that the whole world might envy," he said slowly. "The blood of old France and the blood of a great aboriginal race that is the offshoot of no other race in the world. The Indian blood is a thing of itself, unmixed for thousands of years, a blood that is distinct and exclusive. Few white people can claim such a lineage. Boy, try and remember that as you come of Indian blood, dashed with that of the first great soldiers, settlers and pioneers in this vast Dominion, that you have one of the proudest places and heritages in the world. You are a Canadian in the greatest sense of that great word. When you go out into the world, will you remember that, Fire-Flint?" The Governor's voice ceased, but his thin, pale, aristocratic fingers rested on the boy's shoulder, his eyes still shone with that warm, brotherly light.

"I shall remember, sir," replied Fire-Flint, while his homeless young heart was fast creating for itself the foothold amongst the nations of the earth. The principal stood awkwardly, hoping that all this attention would not spoil his head pupil, but he never knew that boy in all the five years he had instructed him as Lord Mortimer knew him in that five minutes.

"No," said the Governor, turning again to the principal. "I certainly do not like the term 'half-breed.' Most of the people on this continent are of mixed blood — how few are pure English, or pure Scottish or Irish, or indeed of any particular nationality. Yet the white people of mixed blood are never called half-breeds. Why not?"

Then, looking speculatively at Fire-Flint, he asked: "I suppose all the traders use this term in speaking of your parents and of you?"

"Of my parents, yes, sir."

"And you?" The Governor smiled kindly.

"They call me the Shagganappi," said Fire-Flint.

"I'm afraid that's beyond me, my boy. Won't you tell me what it means?"

"It's a buckskin, sir, a colour. A shagganappi cayuse is a buckskin colour. They say I look that way."

"Ah, I understand," replied Lord Mortimer, as his eyes rested on the dark cream brown tint of the boy's face. "Well, it's a good name. Buckskin is a thing essential to white people and to Indians alike, from the Red River to the Rockies. And the cayuse — well, the horse is the noblest animal known to man. So try to be worthy of the nickname, my boy. Live to be essential to your people, like the buckskin, and to be noble, like the horse. And now, goodbye, Shagganappi, and remember always that you are the real Canadian."

Another handclasp, and Lord Mortimer was walking away with the principal at his side.

"You have greatly encouraged that boy, Your Excellency," he said. "I think he always felt terribly that he was a half-bre . . . half-blood. He would have loved to claim either all Cree or all French ancestry."

"He is a fine lad and I like him" returned Lord Mortimer, shortly, for he felt a little impatient with the principal who so easily could have lightened the boy's heart from the first year he had entered school.

First published The Boy's World,
May 19, 1906

Life-Training of
the Redskin Boy-Child.

The Redskin boy-child who looks out from his little cradle-board on a world of forest through whose trails his baby feet are already being fitted to follow is not many hours old before careful hands wrap him about with gay-beaded bands that are strapped to the carven and colored back-board that will cause him to stand erect and upright when he is a grown warrior. His small feet are bound against a foot support so that they are exactly straight; that is to start his walk in life aright.

He is but an atom in the most renowned of the savage races known to history, a people that, according to the white man's standard, is uncivilized, uneducated, illiterate, and barbarous. Yet the upbringing of every Red Indian male child begins at his birth, and ends only when he has acquired the learning considered essential for the successful man to possess, and which has been predetermined through many ages by many wise ancestors.

His education is twofold, and always is imparted in "pairs" of subjects — that is, while he is being instructed in the requisites of fighting, hunting, food getting, and his national sports, he takes with each "subject" a very rigid training in etiquette, for it would be as great a disgrace for him to fail in manners of good breeding as to fail to take the war-path when he reaches the age of seventeen.

FIRST, COURAGE.

The education of an Iroquois boy is begun before he can even speak. The first thing he is taught is courage — the primitive courage that must absolutely despise fear — and at the same time he is thoroughly grounded in the first immutable law of Indian etiquette, which is that under no conceivable conditions must one ever stare, as the Redskin races hold that staring marks the lowest level of ill-breeding.

SECOND, RELIGIOUS TRAINING.

His second subject is religious training. While he is yet a baby in arms he is carried "pick-a-back" in his mother's blanket to the ancient dances and festivals, where he sees for the first time, and in his infant way participates in, the rites and rituals of the pagan faith, learning to revere the "Great Spirit," and to anticipate the happy hunting grounds that await him after death.

At the end of a long line of picturesque braves and warriors who circle gracefully in the worshipping dance, his mother carries him, her smooth, soft-footed, twisting step lulling him to sleep, for his tiny, copper-colored person, swinging to every curve of the dance, soon becomes an unconscious bit of babyhood. But the instant he learns to walk, he learns, too, the religious dance-steps. Then he rises to the dignity of being allowed to slip his hand in that of his father and take his first important steps in the company of the men.

Accompanying his religious training is the all-important etiquette of accepting food without comment. No Indian talks of food, or discusses it while taking it. He must neither commend nor condemn it, and a child who remarks upon the meals set before him, however simple the remark may be, instantly feels his disgrace in the sharpest reproof from his parents. It is one of the unforgivable crimes.

TRICKS OF FOOD-GETTING.

His third subject is to master the tricks of food-getting. His father, or more often his grandfather, takes him in hand at an early age, and minutely trains him in all the art and artifice of the great life-fight for food both for himself and for those who may in later years be dependent on him. He is drilled assiduously in hunting, fishing, trapping, in game calls, in wood and water lore; he learns to paddle with stealth, to step in silence, to conceal himself from the scent and sight of bird and beast, to be swift as a deer, keen as an eagle, alert as a fox.

He is admonished under no conditions, save in that of extreme hunger or in self-defence, to kill mating game, or, in fact, to kill at all save for food or to obtain furs for couch purposes. Wanton slaying of wild things is unknown among the uncivilized Red Indians. When they want occupation in sport or renown, they take the warpath against their fellow-kind, where killing will flaunt another eagle-feather in their crest, not simply another pair of antlers to decorate their tepee.

With this indispensable lesson in the essentials of living always comes the scarcely less momentous one of the utter unimportance of youth. He is untiringly disciplined in the veneration of age, whether it be in man or woman. He must listen with rapt attention to the opinions and advice of the older men. He must keep an absolute silence while they speak, must ever watch for opportunities to pay them deference.

❦ 277

If he happen, fortunately, to be the son of a chief of ancient lineage, the fact that he is of blood royal will not excuse him entering a door before some aged "commoner." Age has more honor than all his patrician line of descent can give him. Those lowly born but richly endowed with years must walk before him; he is not permitted to remain seated if some old employee is standing even at work; his privilege of birth is as nothing compared with the honor of age, even in his father's hireling.

The fourth thing he must master is the thorough knowledge of medicinal roots and herbs — antidotes for snake-bite and poison — also the various charms and the elementary "science" of the medicine man, though the occupation of the latter must be inherited, and made in itself a life study. With this branch of drilling also is inculcated the precept of etiquette never to speak of or act slightingly of another's opinion, and never to say the word "No," which he is taught to regard as a rude refusal. He may convey it by manner or action, but speak it — never.

And during the years he is absorbing this education he is unceasingly instructed in every branch of warfare, of canoe-making, of fashioning arrows, paddles and snowshoes. He studies the sign language, the history and legends of his nation; he familiarizes himself with the "archives" of wampum belts, learning to read them and to value the great treaties they sealed. He excels in the national sports of "lacrosse," "bowl and beans," and "snow snake," and when, finally, he goes forth to face his forest world he is equipped to obtain his own living with wisdom and skill, and starts life a brave, capable, well-educated gentleman, though some yet call him an uncivilized savage.

❧ A SELECTED BIBLIOGRAPHY

WALTER MCRAYE,   *Pauline Johnson and Her Friends,* Ryerson, Toronto, 1947
Town Hall Tonight, Ryerson, Toronto, 1929

HECTOR CHARLESWORTH, *Candid Chronicles,* Macillan, Toronto, 1925

MRS. GARLAND FOSTER,   *The Mohawk Princess,* Lion's Gate Pub. Co., Vancouver, 1931

HORATIO HALE,   *G. H. M. Johnson,* Magazine of American History, Vol. XIII, February, 1885

PAULINE JOHNSON,   *Flint and Feather,* with introduction by Theodore Watts-Dunton, Musson, Toronto, 22nd edition, 1931

JOHN GARVIN,   *Canadian Poets,* McClelland, Toronto, 1916

W. D. LIGHTALL,   *Songs of the Great Dominion,* Scott, Toronto, 1889

Pauline Johnson at age 11.

Her favourite portrait, taken about 1894.